DESIGN ELEMENTS
TYPOGRAPHY
FUNDAMENTALS

© 2012 Rockport Publishers

First published
in the United States of America in 2012
by Rockport Publishers,
a member of Quayside Publishing Group
100 Cummings Center
Suite 406-L
Beverly, Massachusetts 01915-6101
(978) 282-9590 *Telephone*
(978) 283-2742 *Fax*

www.rockpub.com
Visit RockPaperInk.com to share your opinions,
creations, and passion for design.

10 9 8 7 6 5 4 3 2 1

ISBN 978-1-59253-767-9

Digital edition published in 2012
eISBN 978-1-61058-400-5

Library of Congress Cataloging-in-Publication
Data available

Design
Kristin Cullen

Primary Typefaces
Alright Sans, Jackson Cavanaugh, 2009
Epic, Neil Summerour, 2007
Heroic Condensed, Silas Dilworth, 2008

Printed in China

DESIGN ELEMENTS
TYPOGRAPHY
FUNDAMENTALS

a Graphic Style Manual *for understanding how*
TYPOGRAPHY AFFECTS DESIGN

kristin cullen

Rockport Publishers
100 Cummings Center, Suite 406L
Beverly, MA 01915

rockpub.com • rockpaperink.com

CONTENTS

INTRODUCTION

Designers engage with words, typographically expressing them with purpose and poise. Typography is a process, a refined craft making language visible. Designers shape language with type and give words life and power to speak text fluently. Letterforms and their supporting characters are simple shapes that do so much. With distinct voices and personalities, type whispers delicately and shouts loudly. Communication lies at its core. Type is commanding and beautiful one moment, analytic and instructive the next. It is dramatic, whimsical, modest, and extravagant. Typographic practice (and those dedicated to it) gives spoken and written language vitality across time, generations, and cultures.

Rooted in everyday experience, type is ever-present. It often goes unnoticed. Other times, it radiates. A central goal of designers is marrying content and form. Function balances with aesthetics. Boundless methods exist to visualize text with type. Heightened attention and thoughtful articulation are essential. Discipline fosters skill and knowledge. Designing with type for communication challenges and fulfills and continually offers new things to explore.

Design Elements: Typography Fundamentals shares typographic basics. An instructional reader rather than historical survey, it teaches the language of type and typesetting methods. It is not a publication dedicated to software, tools, or technical tips, which evolve at rapid pace. Content focuses on guiding, well-founded principles that endure. They set solid ground on which to design with type across mediums. Limitless potential for meaningful and creative visual communication exists. *Typography Fundamentals* is the field guide for the journey.

May readers, especially students studying typography, gain knowledge and respect for language and typographic design. (With any luck, these pages will also spark a passion for type and typography.) There is so much to delight in and discover.

1

TYPE
IN CONTEXT

"IMMACULATE TYPOGRAPHY IS

certainly the most brittle of all the arts. To create a whole from many petrified,

disconnected and given parts, to make this whole appear alive and of a piece—

only sculpture in stone approaches the unyielding stiffness of perfect typography.

For most people, even impeccable typography does not hold any particular

aesthetic appeal. In its accessibility, it resembles great music. Under the best of

circumstances, it is gratefully accepted. To remain nameless and without specific

appreciation, yet to have been of service to a valuable work and to the small

number of visually sensitive readers—this, as a rule, is the only compensation

for the long, and indeed never-ending, indenture of the typographer."

from "Clay in a Potter's Hand"
The Form of the Book: Essays on the Morality of Good Design

JAN TSCHICHOLD

SELECTED READINGS

The Alphabetic Labyrinth:
The Letters in History and Imagination
Johanna Drucker

Letter Perfect: The Marvelous History
of Our Alphabet from A to Z
David Sacks

A Short History of the Printed Word
Warren Chappell
Robert Bringhurst

Textura
Goudy Text

Rotunda
San Marco

Schwabacher
Duc de Berry

Fraktur
Fette Fraktur

Studying typography starts with ABCs.[1] Letterforms share a heritage with prehistoric cave paintings and early writing systems, notably Sumerian cuneiform and Egyptian hieroglyphs. Over time, sparked by our human need to communicate, pictures of things developed into conceptual marks and sophisticated symbols of sound, which laid the foundation for alphabetic writing systems. Ancient cultures— the Phoenicians, Greeks, Etruscans, and Romans— devised, adapted, and refined alphabets. Thousands of years in the making, the Roman system is our present-day ancestor. Informed by advances of cultures past, it had twenty-three majuscules (uppercase letterforms) with consonants and vowels. (*J*, *U*, and *W* joined the alphabet in the Middle Ages, to mark sounds unneeded earlier.) In *Alphabet: The History, Evolution, and Design of the Letters We Use Today*, Allan Haley writes, "The Roman capitals have had, and still have, the greatest influence on the design and use of capital letters, enduring as the standard of proportion and dignity for almost two thousand years." Minuscules (lowercase letterforms) evolved over hundreds of years, from their origins in handwriting. The late eighth and early ninth centuries saw the making of a standardized minuscule script with enhanced legibility. Called the Carolingian minuscule, it is a key predecessor of the lowercase letterforms we know now. The twenty-six-letter alphabet—the heart of typographic practice—has remained largely unchanged for thousands of years.

In Western civilization, the transition from lettering and handwritten scripts to mechanical typesetting occurred in mid-fifteenth-century Europe, when German-born goldsmith Johannes Gutenberg revolutionized the movable-type printing press. (Movable type was invented by Bi Sheng in China during the 1040s, and printed books using movable type emerged shortly after in Korea.) Gutenberg cast lead alloy movable-type blocks with reusable hand molds. Making almost 300 characters, he replicated calligraphic scripts of the period called Textura, a Blackletter style (named so because of its darkness). With narrow, tightly fitted forms, character strokes are thick and angular.

Gutenberg's durable, individual characters easily reassembled and reprinted on wooden presses. His metal-based ink formula upheld better than water-based precursors. Adhering well to the metal type, the ink made rich blacks with a uniform imprint. Quality mechanization led to efficient production and circulation of text, as well as codified typefaces, which spread across Western culture. Gutenberg's system catapulted type through time— from the Renaissance and Enlightenment to the Victorian Age and Modernism. Contemporary typographers and type designers continue the legacy. Typography endures and progresses with thrilling adventure past, present, and future.

Johannes Gutenberg modeled his first typeface on mid-fifteenth-century calligraphic writing called Textura. It is narrow with tightly fitted characters and dense, angular strokes. Textura is part of a larger Blackletter family that includes Rotunda, Schwabacher, and Fraktur.

1 *Design Elements: Typography Fundamentals* shares typographic basics. An instructional reader, rather than historical survey, it teaches the language of type and typesetting methods. The abridged synopsis here creates context. Histories of alphabets and typography are multifaceted stories. Both offer wisdom and enrich visual communication. Selected readings noted in chapters support further study. See Appendices: Readings (page 148) for a complete list.

DESIGNING WITH TYPE

Projects in all media require distinct typographic use based on function. Merge communication with aesthetics— one without the other limits the potential to convey information effectively and beautifully. Although projects vary with individual needs, follow simple objectives for all when designing with type for communication.

1 *Convey information with type.*
Communicate with clarity.

2 *Assist the reading process.*
Make it accessible (and delightful).

3 *Uphold typeface integrity.*
Value it and its makers.

4 *Express text beautifully.*
Create visually inviting work.

5 *Design with appropriateness.*
Do what best serves each project.

Typography is a process, a refined craft that makes language visible. Designers shape language with type and give words life and power to speak text fluently. With roles semantic and aesthetic, type that expresses text at its best serves both roles at once. Words, lines, and paragraphs carry messages via letterforms. Type conveys information and provokes emotion. It shares stories and influences behavior. At times, typographic characters are abstract constructs or images with no text to communicate, simply beauty made apparent. Typography is not handwriting, calligraphy, or lettering. Only type uses standardized forms that rearrange and reproduce in exact fashion without end. Systematized character sets fit for repeated use with ranges of text distinguish typography from other letter-making methods. Handwriting, calligraphy, and lettering tend to be reserved for customization in limited-edition and special work. Letterforms distinct from available typefaces made by hand or digital tools are unique typographic alternatives.

This vintage-inspired pocket planner, Today Is the Day, includes lovely lettering by designer and illustrator Jessica Hische. Intricate letterforms unique in appearance fill pages. Custom lettering offers one-of-a-kind alternatives to typefaces.

——
GALISON

The stylistic range of calligraphy, which means "beautiful writing," is diverse— from ornate and sinuous to rough and painterly. Tools used, typically a brush or pen, influence appearance. The logotype for Piter Pan, a Ukraine rock band, is handcrafted, then digitally produced.

——
SERGEY SHAPIRO

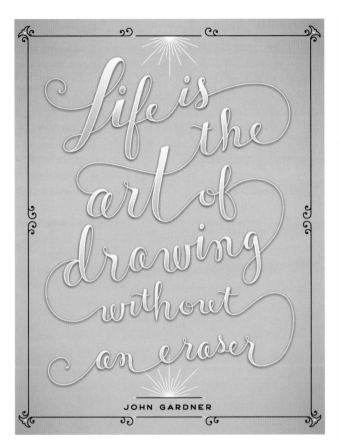

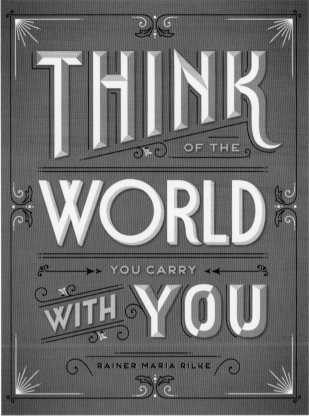

Directional and informational signage
for the luxury hotel Estoi Palace Pousada
is clear and consistently applied in sans
serif Flama. Discreet and functional, it
complements the elegant space.

———

FBA.

Typography is everywhere, crossing mediums
that include environments, interfaces, packaging,
and print. It will no doubt thrive in digital and physical
works to come. Typography is at the center of design
practice. Designing with type for communication
is many-sided. It is analytic and instructive, dramatic
and whimsical. Designers work with type objectively
and subjectively with economy and extravagance.
Environmental signage systems, for example, are
practical and direct; clarity is imperative. Typography
is also conceptual and interpretive. Motion sequences
appeal to viewers through lively type treatments.
Letterforms personify or emote strongly. Regardless
of the medium, balancing function and aesthetics
reigns. Use fundamental principles as the basis to
marry text with type. Do so with appropriateness,
a concept relevant to all things typographic.

Macro- and microtypography describe approaches
to typographic design. Macrotypography addresses
composition or layout—the plan and organization
of typographic elements. Key considerations include
spatial positioning and relationship-building among
elements and white space (negative space). The macro
view is the compositional body, in which designers
order, connect, and balance type. It is the first
impression that engages viewers. Without immediate
visual interest, communication ceases; the intended
typographic messages are not received.

Microtypography refers to typesetting essentials
and details. Designers transform plain text into a typographic system—a hierarchy, with optical emphasis
and strategic variation. Letterform, word, line, and
paragraph dynamics demand acute attention. A principal micro factor is spacing, which includes kerning
and tracking. Aesthetic tailoring, as in refining punctuation and ragging, are other micro components.
Microtypography ensures refined compositions with
considered type settings. Projects are free of distractions and missteps that inhibit reading and communication. The microtypographic level is often undetected
by viewers (a sign of its achievement). Macro- and
microtypography are mutually dependent. The success
of the whole (macro) depends on its parts (micro).

In this student project, choreographed
letterforms perform the song "Que Sera"
by Wax Tailor. The motion sequence
visualizes sound and voice. One-off
typographic arrangements in many typefaces shape scenes. Graphic elements
frame the viewing area and support
typographic action.

———

STROM STRANDELL

Different text in wide-ranging mediums for assorted viewers provides extensive typographic options. Designers might navigate multiple mediums or specialize in one or a limited few. Typography connects all. Numerous spreads with examples and captions follow to exhibit the diversity of typographic practice.

An elegant poster has limited and striking typography. *WB* (Werner Bischof) set in Typonine Stencil is in distinct contrast to the photograph. The color commands attention, and the letterform anatomy defines the alignment of subordinate text. The *B* stem, for example, is the main axis for logos and text, set in sans serif Akzidenz-Grotesk.

—

SENSUS DESIGN FACTORY

Environmental type engages physical space. The permanent installation at the University of Washington School of Business echoes a link between business and change. Typeset in Trade Gothic, stainless-steel letterforms in the stone flooring spell "change" along with synonyms like "adapt," "innovate," and "transform." On each floor, words outside of the elevator doors connect with those inside the elevator. Revealed are phrases such as "global change" and "manage change."

—

KAREN CHENG
KRISTINE MATTHEWS

These expressively illustrated pieces
are fine examples of type as image.
Miscellaneous letterforms interact
playfully. Just one element of a larger
campaign for the bar Le Buro, the
spirited typographic works enchant.

———
INVENTAIRE

Approximately 5,000 letters by composer
Felix Mendelssohn comprise an edition
of books. Book spines feature TheSans
(from the superfamily Thesis) in a range
of weights. A landscape inspired by
Mendelssohn's music in soft shades
of green and yellow appears when the
volumes sit side by side. Connecting
them provides a distinct surprise.

—

TAKE OFF—MEDIA SERVICES

everything is ok

GENERAL WARNING: Global warming. AIDS. Racism. Starvation. Genocide. War. Cancer. Bankruptcy. Illiteracy. Cloning. Republicans. everythingisok.com

Diverse applications from buttons to public spaces comprise the concept-driven campaign Everything is OK. MINE™ explains the project as "a kind of social design experiment in subversive positivism. It explores the relationship between medium and message, challenges accepted modes of communication, and provides everyday citizens with tools for social commentary." A consistent system of color and type— a trio of Helvetica, Trade Gothic, and Dot Matrix—unify elements across mediums.

———

MINE™

The Ramblas Tapas Bar logotype features the typeface Augustus. A speech bubble cleverly replaces the counter of *R* with a second bubble off its leg. The shapes interact and suggest the social exchange that results from sharing many small plates with others versus having one apiece while dining.

———

DAN BECKER

Helvetica capitals present a durable façade in the logotype for Compagnie La Lucette, a boutique real estate company. It stands solidly with modified letterforms like the "ette" in Lucette; the technique links characters and adds unique detail.

———

EURO RSCG C&O

The round forms and clean lines of the typeface Avant Garde shape the logotype for the UK marketing firm Fab. Color and transparency add liveliness and suggest themes of interaction and exchange.

———

EL STUDIO / PETE ROSSI

Type expresses sentiments and creates joy. A collection of everyday letterpress cards reminds us that even simple gestures merit typographic attention. Pictured typefaces include Archer and Futura, as well as a custom face seen in "Word," inspired by Franklin Gothic.

———
WALK UP PRESS

The typeface Akzidenz-Grotesk adds practical charm to the annual report for staffing agency Brunel International. Type size, weight, and color establish hierarchy. The dominant red text is unexpected, sharing brief statistics in an unusual manner. It adds notice and delivers company background boldly.

———
G2K / MATTHIJS VAN LEEUWEN

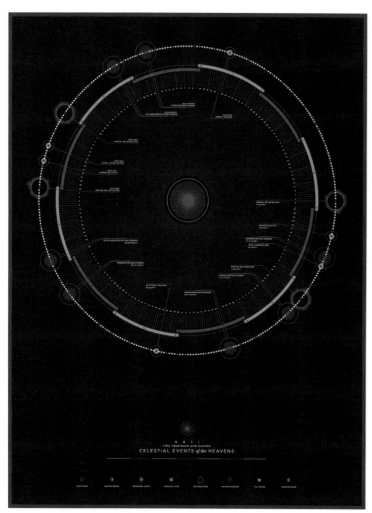

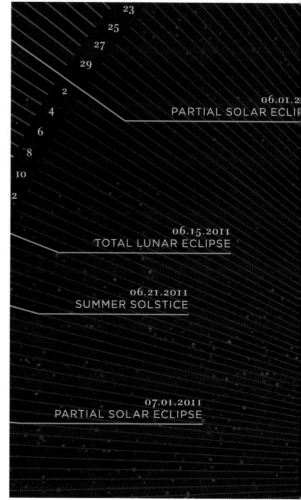

A data-driven poster, titled Celestial
Events of the Heavens, tracks the
moon's cycle and orbit. The subject
matter inspires the radial structure
and deep blue tones. Type settings,
in Centennial and Gotham, are minimal
and elegant. Lines extend like rays and
call out key astral events. Oriented
parallel to the eye, the text is readable from left to right on horizontal,
not angled, baselines.

———
LUKE LANGHUS

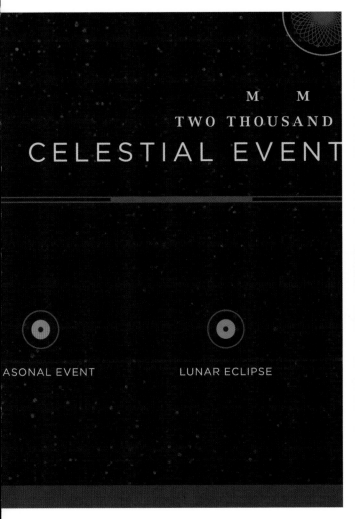

Constructed letterforms creatively
demonstrate an alternate method
of using typefaces. A template set
in the sans serif face Interstate is
the foundation for constructing the
graphic letterforms. The technique
results in an eye-catching poster
for the School of Visual Arts.

———
MIRKO ILIĆ CORP.

The *Fathoms Deep* L P by the Tunnel
displays weathered hand lettering in
the title. The technique integrates text
with image. Delicate type set in Centaur
is quiet and dignified. Red numerals
in Gingko Fraktur add a shot of color.

———

PATRICK L CRAWFORD DESIGN

A bold color palette and delicate pattern set the stage for this simple sans serif and serif combination. The condensed sans serif Chalet Comprimé suggests sureness, and the serif Miller adds polish. The contrast is clear, the information conveyed with ease. A beautiful ampersand adds an extra touch of elegance to the design.

———

NADEN/MESKER DESIGN CO.

The serif typeface Plantin lists design services offered on a promotional mailer. Repurposing antique postcards, type blends with the vintage cards and preserves a historical look. The neutral sans serif Helvetica discreetly conveys contact information.

———

COLLECTIVE APPROACH

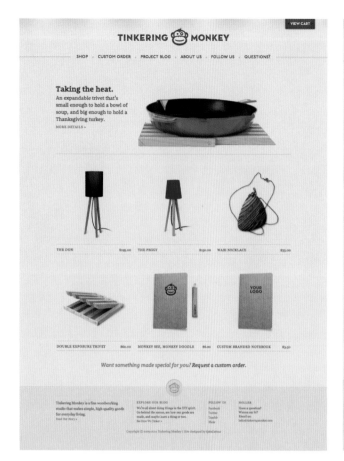

The Tinkering Monkey website is open and accessible. Main navigational links in sans serif Underground lie in the header. An uppercase setting plus color clarifies the site structure. Headings and subheads, such as "Taking the heat" and "We start tinkering," in the serif Rooney Web combine well with Underground. Both typefaces have warm personalities.

—

PAULA CHANG

The package design for Dulce Vida, a 100-proof, 100% organic tequila, is contemporary and tasteful. The brand name in the Blackletter serif Brauhaus Alternate conveys confidence. Direct and refined, the versatile sans serif Flama accompanies the graphic logotype.

—

FOXTROT BRAVO ALPHA (FBA)

2

ESSENTIAL
ELEMENTS

32 *Anatomy & Terminology*

Understanding typography fundamentals includes learning its terminology (the language of type), anatomy (the parts of type), and architecture (the framework of type). Designers share common terms that identify typographic building blocks. Basic terminology is typically constant across mediums, which builds mutual connections from one to another. For example, all typefaces, regardless of their diversity, share anatomical parts and details. A serif is always a serif in digital, print, or environmental projects. Knowing well the parts that comprise typographic practice aids type selection and use. Best expression comes with intimate knowledge of the essential elements, which include characters, measures, and styles. Typographic results arise through the considered manipulation of the essential elements. Cultivating an understanding and gaining proficiency begins with learning basic terminology, anatomy, and architecture.

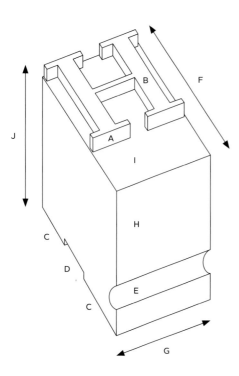

Many typographic terms originate from metal typesetting days when typographers and printers set lead type slugs (cast-metal sorts) by hand to form words, lines, and paragraphs. They shape much of the terminology now used to describe type anatomy and measure.

A   Beard/Bevel
B   Face
C   Feet
D   Groove
E   Nick
F   Point Size/Body Size
G   Set Width
H   Shank
I   Shoulder
J   Type Height/Height to Paper
    0.918 inch (2.3 cm)

A B C D E F G H I J K L M N O P Q R S T U V W X Y Z

a b c d e f g h i j k l m n o p q r s t u v w x y z

A B C D E F G H I J K L M N O P Q R S T U V W X Y Z

fi fl fj ff fb fh fk ffi ffl ffj fff ffb ffh ffk ct st

0 1 2 3 4 5 6 7 8 9

0 1 2 3 4 5 6 7 8 9

¼ ½ ¾ ⁰ ¹ ² ³ ⁴ ⁵ ⁶ ⁷ ⁸ ⁹ ₀ ₁ ₂ ₃ ₄ ₅ ₆ ₇ ₈ ₉

+ < = > | ~ ¬ ± × ÷ ∕ ⁺ ⁻ ⁼ ∂ Δ Π Σ − √ ∞ ∫ ≈ ≠ ≤ ≥

! " # % & ' ( ) * , - . / : ; ? @ [\ ] _ { } ¡ « · » ¿

" ^ ' . , – — ' ' „ " " „ † ‡ • … ‰ ‹ › ? ⁽⁾ ( ) ⟨ ⟩

¦ § © ® ¶ № ᴿᴹ ™ e ↖ ↗ ↘ ↙ $ ¢ £ ¤ ¥ ₵ €

▲ ▶ ▼ ◀ ◉ ◇ ○ ⊗ ◎ ● ◢ ◣ ◤ ◥ ✪ ☠

Select Glyphs
Alright Sans

Glyphs
Glyphs comprise all marks in a typeface from letterforms and numerals to punctuation and symbols. For instance, a diacritic (accent mark) is a glyph, not a character. It combines with a letterform to create a character, as in ´ (acute) + *e* = *é*.

Characters
A character is a typographic element such as a letterform, numeral, or punctuation mark. Typefaces might have multiple versions of each character represented by glyphs. For example, the lowercase *g* character can have three glyphs: single story *g*, double story *g*, and small cap G. The term "alternates" (or alternate characters) applies to the variants.

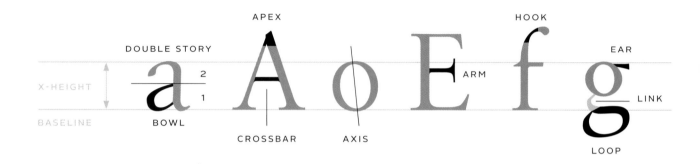

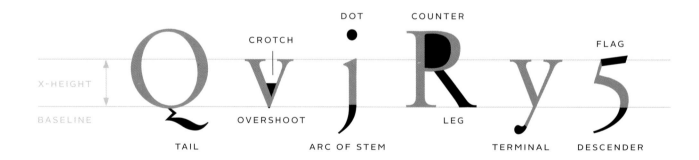

A **Aperture** An aperture (open counter) is the partially enclosed white space in letterforms such as C and S, as well as n and e.

Apex An apex is the top point of a letterform, where two strokes meet, as in A and W.

Arc of Stem An arc of stem is a curved stroke that flows smoothly into a straight stroke. Examples include f, j, and t.

Arm An arm is a short horizontal or vertical stroke attached to another on one end, such as E, F, and L.

Ascender An ascender is the part of lowercase letterforms—b, d, f, h, k, and l— that rises above the x-height.

Axis An axis is the invisible line that bisects character tops and bottoms at the thinnest points. It indicates character stress from oblique to vertical.

B **Bowl** A bowl is the curved character stroke that encloses counters, as seen in a, b, g, and p. Bowls are closed or open, depending on whether or not the curve connects to the stem.

C **Chin** A chin connects the arm and spur of the uppercase G.

Counter A counter (counterform) is the enclosed white space in characters such as b, d, and o. An open counter (aperture) is the partially enclosed white space in characters such as C and S, as well as n and e.

Crossbar A crossbar (cross stroke) is the horizontal bar that connects two strokes (A and H), crosses stems (f and t), or bisects stems (E and F).

Crotch A crotch is the acute inside point where two strokes meet, as in V.

D **Descender** A descender is the part of lowercase letterforms—g, j, p, q, and y— that falls below the baseline.

Dot A dot (tittle) is the rounded mark above the lowercase i and j.

Double story Double story refers to specific letterform variations that have upper and lower closed or open counters. For example, the lowercase g in some typefaces has a bowl plus loop. Another double story letterform is the lowercase a. It features a lower closed bowl with an upper aperture.

E **Ear** An ear is a small stroke that extends from the bowl of the double story lowercase g.

Eye An eye is the closed counter space specific to the lowercase e.

F **Flag** A flag is the horizontal stroke found on the numeral 5.

Finial A finial is the curved and tapered finishing stroke seen in the lowercase a, c, and e.

H **Hook** A hook is the curved stroke in a terminal, as in the lowercase f and r.

L **Leg** A leg is the short, diagonal stroke that sweeps downward in the letterforms K and R.

Link A link is the connecting stroke between the bowl and loop of the double story lowercase g.

Loop A loop is the enclosed or partially enclosed counter of the double story lowercase g. It falls below the baseline and connects via a link to the upper bowl.

O **Overshoot** Overshoot (overhang) is the slight character portion that falls below the baseline or above the cap height or x-height. Examples are A, a, O, o, and V, v. It gives the optical sense that such forms are the same size as those sitting flush on the baseline.

S **Serif** A serif is a small finishing detail at the start and end of strokes.

Shoulder A shoulder is the downward curved stroke that extends off a stem, as in h, m, and n.

Spine A spine is the primary curving stroke of the S.

Spur A spur is a one-sided, small finishing detail that slightly extends from a primary stroke, as in the uppercase E, G, and S.

Stem A stem is the primary vertical stroke of a letterform.

Stroke A stroke is any curved, straight, or diagonal line that constructs characters. Arms, legs, and stems are specific stroke types.

Swash A swash is an embellished stroke that replaces a serif or terminal to create a swash character, a decorative form that is regarded as lively and elegant.

T **Tail** A tail is a downward finishing stroke. The uppercase Q typically features a distinct, often decorative, tail. Uppercase letterforms with legs—like K and R— sometimes have curved tails that fluidly extend from the diagonal stroke.

Terminal A terminal is the curved or straight end of finishing strokes, as seen in a, c, f, j, r, and y. Terminal styles include ball, beak, and teardrop (lachrymal).

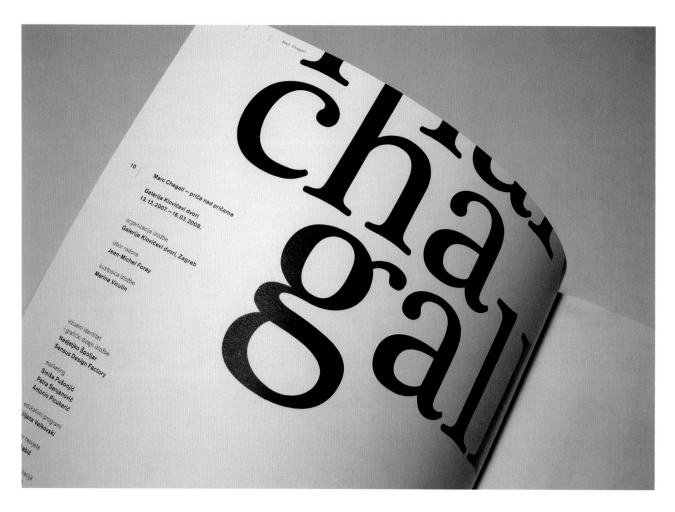

A Marc Chagall monograph detail offers a look at letterform anatomy. Serif Plantagenet Cherokee has the double story letterforms *a* and *g*. Adnate (bracketed) serifs extend fluidly with curved stem connections, as in *h* and *l*—their bottoms are cupped. The *a* and *c* also feature teardrop (lachrymal) terminals.

—

SENSUS DESIGN FACTORY

Par is a book celebrating African Americans who fought segregation to play golf at top levels. The title, set in Gravur Condensed, features modified counters, which are enclosed or partially enclosed white spaces in characters that aid legibility. Such a look creates a clean diecut without sacrificing readability.

—

BLØK DESIGN

MARIOLA ANDONEGUI ARTE CULTURA PATRIMONIO

The Mariola Andonegui Arte Cultura Patrimonio logotype activates letter-form counters. The extracted counter spaces from the typeface Century Gothic provide graphic notice. The method deepens the aesthetic and adds dynamic effect.

—

LSDSPACE

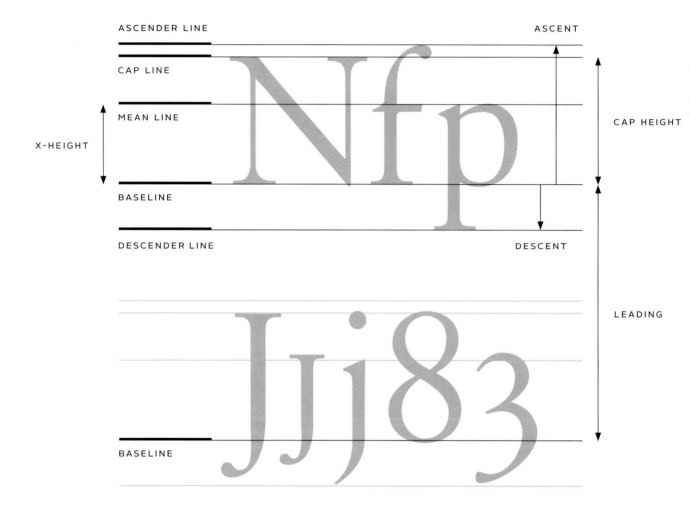

ASCENDER LINE

ASCENT

CAP LINE

MEAN LINE

X-HEIGHT

CAP HEIGHT

BASELINE

DESCENDER LINE

DESCENT

LEADING

BASELINE

A *Ascender Line* The ascender line marks the height or highest point of ascenders.

Ascent Ascent is the maximum letterform height from the baseline beyond the cap line.

B *Baseline* The baseline is the imaginary line on which letterforms, words, lines, and paragraphs sit.

C *Cap Height* Cap height is the distance from the baseline to cap line that measures uppercase letterform height (without diacritics).

Cap Line The cap line marks the height or highest point of uppercase letterforms.

D *Descender Line* The descender line marks the lowest point of descenders.

Descent Descent is the maximum letterform distance below the baseline.

L *Leading* Leading (line spacing) is the vertical distance from one baseline to the next measured in points. The term derives from metal typesetting days when lead strips were set between lines of type to adjust vertical spacing.

M *Mean Line* The mean line (mid line) marks the height or highest point of lowercase letterforms minus ascenders and descenders.

X *X-height* X-height is the distance from baseline to mean line, or, typically, the top of the lowercase *x*. It measures lowercase letterform height minus ascenders and descenders. X-height conveys perceived typeface size.

BASELINE ALIGNMENT

Baselines are imaginary lines on which letterforms, words, lines, and paragraphs sit. Baseline alignment refers to a calculated system of horizontal guides at equally spaced vertical intervals that underlie typographic layouts. A baseline alignment system designates related positions for all type, no matter the range of point sizes. Baselines enable consistent horizontal alignment across compositions. Lines of type coincide; they also back up from page-to-page if viewed one atop another (see chapter 5).

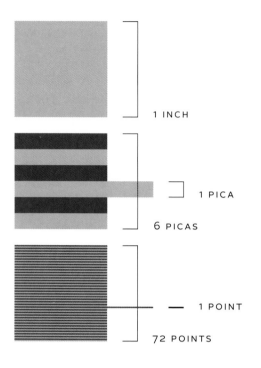

1 pica = 12 points = 0.166 inch (4.2 mm)
6 picas = 72 points = 1 inch (2.5 cm)

1 point = 0.0138 inch (0.35 mm)
12 points = 1 pica = 0.166 inch (4.2 mm)
72 points = 6 picas = 1 inch (2.5 cm)

Em
An em is a typographic measure equal to the point size (type size) used. An em in a 6-point typeface is 6 point; in a 12-point typeface it is 12 point.

6-point em

12-point em

En
An en is a typographic measure equal to half an em. An en in an 8-point type-face is 4 point, in a 16-point typeface it is 8 point.

4-point en

8-point en

Pica
A pica (abbreviated *p*) is a typographic measure equal to 12 points. Picas measure line length.

Point
A point (abbreviated *pt*) is a typographic measure equal to 0.0138 inch (0.35 mm). Points measure type size and leading (line spacing).

Point Size
Point size (type size) refers to the body size of a character—not its appearing size. Typefaces that share matching point sizes do not always have the same optical size. For example, same-sized typefaces with tall x-heights (the distance from baseline to mean line, or, typically, the top of the lowercase *x*) look larger than faces with small x-heights.

Body Size
Body size is the area a character inhabits plus added white space surrounding it. Body height equals point size. The term body size originates in metal-typesetting days when lead-type blocks called slugs (or cast-metal sorts) contained characters. Lead slugs had bases slightly larger than the character size.

Appearing Size
Appearing size refers to optical size or perceived character size; 12-point type in one face might look larger or smaller than the same measure in other typefaces.

Sidebearings
Digital characters have slight white spaces on their left and right sides called sidebearings. Defining the distance between characters, side-bearings are substantial factors in typeface design. The term *set width* refers to the combined width of the character and sidebearings.

110-point Type Size
Epic and Alright Sans

CHARACTER WIDTH

SET WIDTH

Jenson

Bembo

Baskerville

Didot

Rockwell

Univers

Jenson

Baskerville

Clarendon

Akzidenz-Grotesk

Contrast

Contrast refers to the relationship between thick and thin strokes. Serif typefaces such as Bodoni and Didot have a high thick-to-thin stroke contrast. Sans serif typefaces such as Trade Gothic and Univers feature a low to uniform thick-to-thin stroke contrast.

Stress

Stress refers to the invisible axis that bisects character tops and bottoms at the thinnest points. Orientation is oblique or vertical. Stress is detectible using the lowercase *o* as a guide.

Serif

A serif is a small finishing detail at the start and end of strokes. Basic serif constructions are reflexive and transitive; bilateral and unilateral; abrupt and adnate. Variants include cupped, hairline, rounded, slab, and wedge. The first roman serif typefaces appeared in the fifteenth century. Typifying the Humanist typeface category, the style was inspired by Italian handwriting called "lettera antica." Other serif typeface categories include Old Style, Transitional, Modern, and Slab (see chapter 3).

Sans Serif

Sans serif refers to type without serifs and very low to uniform thick-to-thin stroke contrast. The first known sans serif typeface by William Caslon IV appeared in 1816. Vincent Figgins coined the term sans serif roughly twenty years later. Sans serif typeface categories are Grotesque, Geometric, Humanist, and Transitional (see chapter 3).

a b c

Aa Bb Cc Dd Ee Ff Gg Hh Ii
Jj Kk Ll Mm Nn Oo Pp Qq Rr
Ss Tt Uu Vv Ww Xx Yy Zz
0 1 2 3 4 5 6 7 8 9

Serif
Epic

a b c

Aa Bb Cc Dd Ee Ff Gg Hh Ii
Jj Kk Ll Mm Nn Oo Pp Qq Rr
Ss Tt Uu Vv Ww Xx Yy Zz
0 1 2 3 4 5 6 7 8 9

Sans Serif
Alright Sans

Abrupt
Bilateral
Reflexive

Abrupt
Unilateral
Reflexive

Adnate
Bilateral
Reflexive

Adnate
Unilateral
Reflexive

Adnate
Unilateral
Transitive

Cupped

Hairline

Rounded

Slab

Wedge

Serifs are small finishing details at the start and end of strokes. Serif constructions are reflexive and transitive; bilateral and unilateral; abrupt and adnate. Cupped, hairline, rounded, slab, and wedge are serif variations.

Abrupt Serif
Abrupt (unbracketed) serifs extend sharply with angled stem connections.

Adnate Serif
Adnate (bracketed) serifs extend fluidly with curved stem connections.

Bilateral Serif
Bilateral serifs extend off both sides of the stroke.

Unilateral Serif
Unilateral serifs extend off one side of the stroke.

Reflexive Serif
Reflexive serifs break slightly at the stroke then continue off it. They are typically evident in roman typefaces.

Transitive Serif
Transitive serifs flow smoothly out of the stroke without pause. They are typically evident in italic typefaces and most often unilateral.

TYPEFACE, FONT, SUPERFAMILY

A typeface is the consistent design, or distinct visual form, of a type family. It is a cohesive system of related shapes created by a type designer. Characters such as letterforms, numerals, and punctuation share formal attributes. In metal typesetting days, a font was a complete character set of a typeface in one point size and style—12-point Centaur roman, for example. A font can also describe family members comprising typefaces such as light, regular, and bold. For instance, Bembo is a typeface, Bembo italic a font. Digitally speaking, font refers to a computer file that makes a typeface available for use and production. Superfamilies are full-bodied typeface families that can include serif, semi serif, sans serif, semi sans, and slab serif faces. Extensive weights and widths, as well as optical styles, are common. Unified by concept and form, superfamilies add unique flavor to typographic works, all connected by family ties. See chapter 3 for more on typefaces.

Uppercase
Uppercase refers to capital letterforms (majuscules). They share uniform heights called cap height. The term uppercase originates from letterpress printing. Sectioned type cases held uppercase and lowercase slugs; uppercase forms sat in the upper part.

Lowercase
Lowercase refers to small letterforms (minuscules). They differ from uppercase in that they have more variation in form, as well as ascenders and descenders, which aid readability. The term lower-case originates from letterpress printing. Sectioned type cases held uppercase and lowercase slugs; lowercase forms sat in the lower part.

Small Caps
Small caps are uniquely designed uppercase letterforms that share with lowercase a similar weight and x-height (small caps are typically slightly taller). When elements such as acronyms and abbreviations are in body text, small caps replace full capitals, which are optically too large next to lowercase letterforms. Use small caps only if offered in a selected typeface—not all contain them. Reducing full caps to small-cap size makes them look too thin and narrow. "Fake small caps" are awkward and discordant.

A B C

Uppercase

a b c

Lowercase

A B C

Small Caps

Aa **123**

Proportional Lining

Aa **123**

Proportional Non-lining

Aa **123**

Tabular Lining

Aa **123**

Tabular Non-lining

Aa **123**

Inferiors

Aa **123**

Superiors

Lining Figures
Lining figures (titling figures) are numerals that are the same height as uppercase letterforms. Unlike non-lining figures, they do not have ascenders or descenders. Lining figures are well suited in combination with full capitals.

Non-lining Figures
Non-lining figures (old-style or text figures) are numerals with variable widths, ascenders, and descenders. Some sit on the baseline (0, 1, 2, 6, 8); others fall below it (3, 4, 5, 7, 9). They share weight and x-height with lowercase letterforms and small caps. Non-lining figures serve body and continuous text well. They blend fittingly with lowercase without commanding attention like lining figures, which are hulking in such situations and disrupt fluid reading.

Proportional Figures
Proportional figures are numerals with variable width or body size. For instance, the numeral 1 has a narrower width than the numeral 3. They accommodate many texts except numerical data or columns of numerals that require vertical alignment (in which case, tabular figures are apt). Proportional figures may be lining or non-lining.

Tabular Figures
Tabular figures are monospaced numerals, meaning all share the same character width or fixed width. They accommodate numerical data or columns of numerals that require vertical alignment, as in tables or charts. Tabular figures may be lining or non-lining.

Inferiors and Superiors
Inferiors and superiors are small characters used for special text such as footnotes, mathematical notations, and scientific formulas. Inferiors (subscripts) fall below the baseline. Superiors (superscripts) rise above the baseline and hang from or top-align to the ascender line. Inferiors and superiors are specially designed and proportioned forms, not reduced full-size characters, which appear too thin when scaled.

Analphabetics are characters used with the alphabet and are not included in its alphabetic order (or ABCs). They include punctuation, diacritics (accent or diacritical marks), and symbols. Punctuation marks clarify text structure and meaning. Common examples are apostrophes, commas, and periods. Diacritics, such as acute (´), circumflex (ˆ), and umlaut (¨), are auxiliary marks that combine with letterforms and indicate a distinct sound or vocal emphasis. Symbols, such as arithmetical and currency signs, as well as copyright and registered marks, are special-purpose characters.

SELECTED READINGS

The Chicago Manual of Style
The University of Chicago Press

The Typographic Desk Reference
Theodore Rosendorf

Punctuation

〈 〉	angle brackets
' '	apostrophe (single quote)
*	asterisk
•	bullet
|	bar (pipe)
¦	broken bar
:	colon
,	comma
{ }	curly brackets
†	dagger
‡	double dagger
…	ellipsis
—	em dash
–	en dash
!	exclamation mark
¡	inverted exclamation mark
‹ › « »	guillemets
-	hyphen
‽	interrobang
·	midpoint
( )	parentheses
.	period (full stop)
′ ″	prime and double prime
?	question mark
¿	inverted question mark
" "	quotation marks
;	semicolon
/	solidus
\	reverse solidus
[ ]	square brackets

Arithmetical Signs

÷	divide
=	equal
∞	infinity
−	minus
×	multiply
%	percent
+	plus
±	plus-minus
√	radical
≠	unequal

Symbols

&	ampersand
@	at
©	copyright
¤	currency
¢	cent
₡	colón
$	dollar
€	euro
£	pound
¥	yen
°	degree
✪	dingbat
µ	micro, mu
#	octothorp (hash mark)
¶	pilcrow
®	registered
§	section
™	trademark

Diacritics

Á Ő	´ ˝	acute and double acute
Û û	ˆ	arch
Ĕ ğ	˘	breve
Ǩ ř	ˇ	caron
Ç ş	¸	cedilla
Ŷ ŵ	ˆ	circumflex
Ė ṅ	·	dot above (overdot)
À è	` ̏	grave and double grave
Ā ī	¯	macron
Ą ę	˛	ogonek
Å ů	°	ring
	ə	schwa
Ã ỹ	~	tilde
Ü ẅ	¨	umlaut (diaeresis)
Ţ ş	،	undercomma
Ṭ ṛ	.	underdot
ẖ ḥ	_	lowline

Posture
Univers 55 Regular, 56 Oblique

Weight
Univers 45 Light, 55 Regular, 65 Bold, 75 Black

Width
Univers 53 Extended, 55 Regular, 57 Condensed, 59 Ultra Condensed

USING TYPE STYLES

Use only available styles—posture, weight, and width—of chosen typefaces; these have been carefully considered and proportioned by type designers. Avoid relying on software conversions or manual modifications; select italic or oblique fonts from within the type-face. Avoid modifying roman styles by slanting, thus creating objectionable "fake italics." Adding strokes to vary type weight is poor practice. Equally so is skewing or stretching letterforms to make narrow or wide alternatives, which diminish proper proportions and typeface integrity. Choose typefaces with a stylistic range that best meets needs. Those fittingly selected and expressed with skilled treatment produce quality outcomes.

Style is typeface posture, weight, and width.

Posture
Posture is the angle of letterforms relative to the baseline. Roman letterforms are upright with a vertical stance. (The term roman also refers to the regular weight of a typeface.) Posture also includes italics and obliques, which typically sit at a 12- to 15-degree slant from the roman position.

Derived from handwriting, the first italic appeared in Italy during the fifteenth century. Venetian printer Aldus Manutius introduced the style as an alternative to roman body text. Used in pocket-sized books, the narrower italic form allowed more words per line, which saved space and money. Italics and obliques now create emphasis within roman text rather than acting as substitutes for it. They are precise in construction and proportion. Serif typefaces typically have true italics—harmonious partners to romans with structurally different designs. Sans serifs traditionally feature obliques, which are aptly sloped versions of roman forms. Many contemporary sans serifs have true italics, and some serifs have obliques.

Weight
Weight refers to stroke thickness. Regular (book or roman) and bold are traditional weights common to most typefaces. Additional weights include thin, light, medium, black, and ultra.

Width
Width (how wide the letterforms stand) indicates horizontal letterform proportion. Condensed is a typical width narrow in appearance. Compressed and extra-condensed are others. Extended refers to widths with markedly broad appearances.

Identity materials for Emigre Film feature the non-lining numerals 5 and 2. Set in the serif face Matrix, the elegant numerals contrast with the remaining text, which appears in sans serifs Trade Gothic, Citizen, and Antitled. Such typeface distinction makes 52 a focal point, even though it is small in scale next to Emigre.

———

BLØK DESIGN

Letterforms, diacritics, and punctuation marks provide meaning and curiosity on the *Temas de Psicanálise* (*Themes of Psychoanalysis*) covers. The characters, set in Century Schoolbook, are key elements serving as personified graphics that support book titles.

———

FBA.

Inspired by Constructivism, promotional materials for Glasgow rock band Sindûstry are bold in execution. A circumflex (^) above the *U* is for graphic effect not pronunciation. The diacritic is structurally sharp. It is a distinct visual note—typographic form used with dramatic intent. The typeface is Helvetica Ultra Condensed.

———

PETE ROSSI

A ligature is the union of two or more characters. Varieties include stylistic, lexical, and discretionary.

Stylistic Ligatures
Stylistic ligatures resolve unwanted character collisions that occur when certain letterforms combine. Such ligatures deliver aesthetic refinement. Common examples are *fi*, *ffi*, and *fl*.

Lexical Ligatures
Lexical ligatures (diphthongs) represent composite vowels such as *æ* (aesc) and *œ* (ethel).

Discretionary Ligatures
Several typefaces also contain discretionary ligatures. They add stylistic grace with ornate or historical nuance. Options include *ct* and *st*.

Ampersand
Another ligature is the ampersand, which symbolizes the Latin word *et*, meaning "and." Some ampersand variations clearly echo their heritage as *e* and *t* ligatures; others vary indirectly, with little *e* and *t* resemblance.

Stylistic Ligatures

Lexical Ligatures

Discretionary Ligatures

Ampersands

Logik

Carissa Pelleteri

The Logik logotype conveys connections via a custom *gi* ligature, which also unites with the *k*. It is apt for a company that analyzes text documents and reveals links among them. The modified typeface is Century Schoolbook.

idAPOSTLE

A specially designed *ri* ligature enriches the aesthetic and personality of the Carissa Pelleteri logotype, which is set in Austin Bold. A modified *r* terminal replaces the dot (tittle) of the *i* and shapes the letterform.

JESSE REED

Swash characters *a* and *e* in the serif Minion add elegance to the Havana advertisement. The *st* discretionary ligature in "Lifestyle" fits well with the swash characters and ties together the treatment. The embellished letterforms also contrast with the geometric background and sans serif typeface Rimouski. Such visual distinction adds prominence.

FACE.

3

ON
TYPEFACES

A   B   C   D   E

F   G   H   I   J

K   L   M   N   O

P   Q   R   S   T

Typefaces exist in many shapes, which can make unending configurations. Anything imagined is available—from alphabetic and decorative to symbolic and experimental. With many choices, make quality selections and use what exists with discipline and skill.

A   Blackletter
Halja, Michael Parson, 2008

B   Brush Lettering
Filmotype Atlas, Charles Gibbons, 2011

C   Calligraphic
Alana, Laura Worthington, 2011

D   Chromatic
Rosewood, Carl Crossgrove, Kim Buker Chansler, Carol Twombly, 1994

E   Distressed
Stomper, Matthew Aaron Desmond, 1997

F   Experimental
Hunter, Si Scott, 2009

G   Incised
Albertus, Berthold Wolpe, 1932–1940

H   Mathematical
Universal Mathematical Pi, Linotype Design Studio, 1990

I   Monospaced
Orator, John Scheppler, 1962

J   Ornamental
Adobe Wood Type Ornaments, Barbara Lind, Joy Redick, 1990

K   Pixellated
Pixeleite, Rafael Neder, 2005

L   Period/Retro
Peignot, A.M. Cassandre, 1937

M   Sans Serif
Heroic, Silas Dilworth, 2008

N   Serif
Newzald, Kris Sowersby, 2008

O   Slab Serif
Caecilia, Peter Matthias Noordzij, 1990

P   Stencil
ARGN, Greg Ponchak, 2011

Q   Symbol
Carta, Lynne Garell, 1986

R   Typewriter
American Typewriter, Joel Kaden, Tony Stan, 1974

S   Unicase
Democratica, Miles Newlyn, 1991

T   Wood Type
Quentin, URW Studio, 2008

The terms *typeface* and *font* are commonly interchanged (and occasionally disputed). A typeface is the consistent design, or distinct visual form, of a type family. It is a cohesive system of related shapes created by a type designer. Characters, such as letterforms, numerals, and punctuation, share formal attributes.

Font has multiple definitions. In metal typesetting days, a font was a complete character set of a typeface in one point size and style, such as 12-point Centaur roman. A font can also describe family members comprising typefaces, such as light, regular, and bold. For instance, Bembo is a typeface, but Bembo italic is a font. Digitally speaking (and in common practice), font refers to a computer file that makes a typeface available for use and production. A font scalable to any point size embodies the design of a typeface. Designers select typefaces and work with fonts.

Typefaces influence communication through appearance and legibility. Aesthetics provide first impressions and express personalities, such as friendly, professional, or sweet and youthful, masculine, or utilitarian. Connotation, or implied meaning, inherent in typefaces plays a significant role, be it positive or negative. Apt typefaces directly engage viewers and send convincing messages. Legibility refers to the recognition of single characters and their relationships when set side by side. Type designers carefully construct characters and pay special attention to space, notably counters and sidebearings. Counters are enclosed or partially enclosed white spaces in characters, sidebearings the built-in space on their left and right sides. Character shape plus white space (counters and sidebearings) aid letterform recognition. Legibility relies on the invisible presence of space. Choose legible typefaces and—with attentive typesetting— shape readable text. Some typefaces intentionally challenge legibility. Artistry and expression drive utility, not communication. It is exciting to see such creativity for lovers of letterforms!

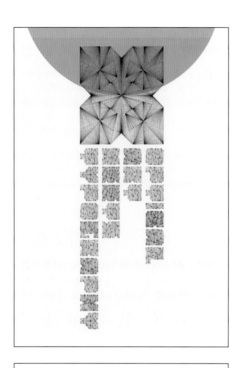

Typefaces are key tools of visual communication. Designers assemble language and form with them. Applied adeptly, typefaces create lasting effects. Take care when handling them, and respect their makers. Invest in them, and gradually build a quality typeface library. Stated gracefully by mid-twentieth-century designer Will Burtin: "Each typeface is a piece of history, like a colored stone chip in a mosaic that depicts the development of human communication. Each typeface is also a visual record of the person who created it— his skill as a designer, his philosophy as an artist, his feeling for the relationship between the details of each letter, and the resulting impressions of an alphabet or a text line." [1] Typefaces are indispensable; they conduct visible language.

1   Rosen, Ben.
    Type and Typography: The Designer's Type Book. Rev. ed.
    New York: Van Nostrand Reinhold Company, 1976.

Simple geometric shapes are the basis of Shape Font. Intended for use in headlines and titles, the typeface challenges legibility. The vertical-reading phrase "Optical Art Meets Typography" captures the concept behind the design.

———

RUI RIBEIRO

A graphic typeface pushes legibility on a poster that promotes an experimental type lecture at the University of Texas at Arlington. The designer states: "The modular typeface is composed entirely and ludicrously of circles and provides a playful visual play of form, counterform, legibility, and illegibility." The top portion of the poster delivers lecture details, the bottom, the key from A–Z and 0–9.

———

TORE TERRASI

SELECTED READINGS

The Elements of Typographic Style
Robert Bringhurst

Manuel français de typographie moderne
Francis Thibaudeau

Printing Types: An Introduction
Alexander S. Lawson

"Type Classification"
*Twentieth Century Graphic Communication:
Technology, Society and Culture*
Annual Conference of the Friends of
St Bride Printing Library, London
Catherine Dixon

Identifying and organizing more than 550 years of typography and myriad typefaces is a challenging task (not without debate among typophiles) that has been taken on by many throughout the years, including Francis Thibaudeau, Maximilien Vox, Alexander Lawson, Robert Bringhurst, and Catherine Dixon. Classification began in the nineteenth century, by printers seeking to note lineage and classify typefaces during a period marked by many new styles. Various classification systems exist, each with organizational methods based on factors such as historical development, formal attributes, and intended use. These methods are points of departure, not perfect plans. Many typefaces fit easily in categories; others overlap in multiple ways or escape classification entirely. Regardless of the system (and the limitations of each), cataloging typefaces is a valuable exercise. Classification shapes context and provides descriptive terms, which aids general identification and selection.

Presented here is a scheme that provides a basic means of identifying and distinguishing typefaces for beginning readers. Dedicated only to serifs and sans serifs suited for most text, it is not a comprehensive model covering all typefaces. Formal traits and historical development shape the fundamental typeface categories: 1. *Serif*—Humanist, Old Style, Transitional, and Modern; 2. *Slab Serif*—Egyptian and Clarendon; and 3. *Sans Serif*—Grotesque, Geometric, Humanist, and Transitional.

Ae
Co

Ae
Co

CATEGORIES

SERIF
Humanist
Old Style
Transitional
Modern

SLAB SERIF
Egyptian
Clarendon

SANS SERIF
Grotesque
Geometric
Humanist
Transitional

HUMANIST SERIF

First Appeared
Fifteenth century

Archetype
Jenson
Nicolas Jenson, 1470

Humanist serifs are the original roman typefaces. They are strikingly different from Blackletter, the first typeface style (see chapter 1). Inspired by Italian handwriting, called "lettera antica," Humanist serifs have a low thick-to-thin stroke contrast and bracketed serifs. The lowercase *e* features an angled, rather than horizontal, crossbar. Round forms such as *o* have an oblique stress.

Typical Characteristics
· Low thick-to-thin stroke contrast
· Oblique stress
· Angled crossbar on the lowercase *e*
· Bracketed serifs
· Small x-height

Examples
· Centaur
  Bruce Rogers, 1915
· Guardi
  Reinhard Haus, 1986
· Lynton
  Leslie Usherwood, 1980
· Maiola
  Veronika Burian, 2005
· Vendetta
  John Downer, 1999

OLD STYLE SERIF

First Appeared
Fifteenth and sixteenth centuries

Archetype
Bembo
Francesco Griffo, 1495

Old Style serifs are more refined, with smoother and rounder forms than Humanist serifs. Because of improvements in type-making tools, the thick-to-thin stroke contrast is more apparent. The crossbar of the lowercase *e* is horizontal. The stress of the *o* shifts vertically, though not fully so.

Typical Characteristics
· Medium thick-to-thin stroke contrast
· Oblique stress
· Horizontal crossbar on the lowercase *e*
· Bracketed serifs
· Round open characters

Examples
· Aldus Nova
  Hermann Zapf, Akira Kobayashi, 2005
· Berling
  Karl-Erik Forsberg, 1951–1958
· Galliard
  Matthew Carter, 1978
· Granjon
  George William Jones, 1928
· Sabon
  Jan Tschichold, 1967

Ae Co

TRANSITIONAL SERIF

First Appeared
Eighteenth century

Archetype
Baskerville
John Baskerville, 1754

Inspired by engraving, Transitional serif characters are mechanical in construction, with medium to high thick-to-thin stroke contrast. Bracketed serifs are sharper and refined—far more than Humanist and Old Style serifs, yet not extreme, like forthcoming Modern typefaces. Round characters are open, with tall x-heights. Vertical stress on round forms is barely oblique to vertical.

Typical Characteristics
· Medium to high thick-to-thin stroke contrast
· Slight oblique to vertical stress
· Horizontal crossbar on the lowercase *e*
· Moderately thin bracketed serifs
· Round open characters
· Tall x-height

Examples
· Arnhem
  Fred Smeijers, 2002
· Bonesana
  Matthieu Cortat, 2009
· Fournier
  Pierre Simon Fournier, 1924
· Photina
  José Mendoza y Almeida, 1971
· Whitman
  Kent Lew, 2003–2008

Ae Co

MODERN SERIF

First Appeared
Eighteenth century

Archetype
Didot
Firmin Didot, 1784

Modern serif typefaces have a very high thick-to-thin stroke contrast. Advances in letterform making and printing methods made possible the superfine and now unbracketed horizontal serifs that typify Moderns. With vertical stress, characters are well balanced and noticeably upright, with slightly condensed proportions.

Typical Characteristics
· Very high thick-to-thin stroke contrast
· Vertical stress
· Horizontal crossbar on the lowercase *e*
· Hairline unbracketed serifs
· Tall x-height

Examples
· Ambroise
  Jean François Porchez, 2001
· Carmen
  Andreu Balius, 2007–2008
· Eloquent
  Jason Walcott, 2008
· Moderno F B
  David Berlow with Richard Lipton, 1995
· Walbaum
  Justus Erich Walbaum, 1800

Ae Co

EGYPTIAN SLAB SERIF

First Appeared
Nineteenth century

Archetype
Rockwell
Frank Hinman Pierpont, 1934

Egyptian slab serif typefaces have a very low thick-to-thin or uniform stroke contrast. Heavy and square unbracketed serifs easily identify them. Historically, their heft worked well as display faces, notably for advertising. Contemporary slabs are typically more versatile than past models. For example, Archer by Hoefler & Frere-Jones has many weights and true italics that serve body-to-display text well.

Typical Characteristics
· Very low to uniform thick-to-thin stroke contrast
· Vertical stress
· Horizontal crossbar on the lowercase *e*
· Square unbracketed serifs

Examples
· Archer
  Hoefler & Frere-Jones, 2008
· Caecilia
  Peter Matthias Noordzij, 1990
· Calvert
  Margaret Calvert, 1980
· Dispatch
  Cyrus Highsmith, 1999–2000
· Memphis
  Rudolf Wolf, 1929

Ae Ae
Co Co

CLARENDON SLAB SERIF

First Appeared
Nineteenth century

Archetype
Clarendon
Robert Besley, 1845

Clarendon slab serifs feature bracketed serifs and low thick-to-thin stroke contrast. Serifs smoothly transition into strokes, a detail making Clarendons appear more refined than Egyptians. A distinct trait is the bulbous ball terminals seen on characters such as lowercase *c*, *f*, and *y*.

Typical Characteristics
· Low thick-to-thin stroke contrast
· Vertical stress
· Horizontal crossbar on the lowercase *e*
· Square bracketed serifs
· Round ball terminals

Examples
· Egizio
Aldo Novarese, 1955
· Oxtail
Stefan Hattenbach, 2006
· Stag
Christian Schwartz, 2006
· Trilby
David Jonathan Ross, 2009
· Volta
Konrad F. Bauer, Walter Baum, 1956

GROTESQUE SANS SERIF

First Appeared
Nineteenth century

Archetype
Akzidenz-Grotesk
Günter Gerhard Lange, 1898

Grotesque styles were the first commercially widespread sans serif typefaces—specific to the late nineteenth and early twentieth centuries. They show little to uniform thick-to-thin stroke contrast. Curved strokes on letterforms such as *c*, *e*, and *s* end at an angle. Grotesque typefaces inspired Transitional sans serifs, which date from the mid-twentieth century. Bureau Grot (1989–2006) and Bau (2001–2004) are contemporary typefaces based on Grotesques.

Typical Characteristics
· Slight thick-to-thin stroke contrast
· Vertical stress
· Curved strokes like *C* end at an angle

Examples
· Basic Commercial
Linotype Design Studio, 1900
· Bell Gothic
Chauncey H. Griffith, 1937
· Franklin Gothic
Morris Fuller Benton, 1904
· Monotype Grotesque
Frank Hinman Pierpont, 1926
· Scheltersche Grotesk
Schelter & Giesecke Foundry, 1880

Ae Co

GEOMETRIC SANS SERIF

First Appeared
Twentieth century

Archetype
Futura
Paul Renner, 1928

Geometry and modularity inspire Geometric sans serif typefaces. Typically based on circles, squares, or triangles, they are rational in construction with uniform stroke contrast.

Typical Characteristics
- Uniform stroke contrast
- Vertical stress
- Inspired by geometric shapes

Examples
- Avant Garde
  Herb Lubalin, Tom Carnase, 1970
- Brandon Grotesque
  Hannes von Döhren, 2009–2010
- Bryant
  Eric Olson, 2002
- Mostra Nuova
  Mark Simonson, 2009
- Neutraface
  Christian Schwartz, 2002

HUMANIST SANS SERIF

First Appeared
Twentieth century

Archetype
Gill Sans
Eric Gill, 1927–1930

Humanist sans take their inspiration from Humanist serifs. A handwritten influence is evident by the slightly more (though subtle) thick-to-thin stroke contrast, which distinguishes them from other sans serif typefaces. Typically, Humanist sans serifs feature true italics distinct from romans.

Typical Characteristics
- Very low thick-to-thin or uniform stroke contrast
- Slight oblique to vertical stress
- Calligraphic influence
- True italics

Examples
- Agenda
  Greg Thompson, 1993–2000
- Elido
  Sibylle Hagmann, 2010
- Leska
  Alexandra Korolkova, 2008
- Mr Eaves
  Zuzana Licko, 2009
- Neue Sans
  André Leonardt, 2007

TRANSITIONAL SANS SERIF

First Appeared
Twentieth century

Archetype
Univers
Adrian Frutiger, 1957

From the mid-twentieth century on, Transitional sans serifs began as refreshed Grotesques, which are specific to the late nineteenth and early twentieth centuries. Characters feature uniform stroke contrast and vertical stress. Early Transitional sans serifs, such as Helvetica and Univers, have curved letterforms such as *c*, *e*, and *s* that end horizontally rather than an angle. Oblique italics are common.

Typical Characteristics
- Uniform stroke contrast
- Vertical stress
- Neutral personality
- Curved strokes like *C* end horizontally

Examples
- Aktiv Grotesk
  Ron Carpenter, Fabio Haag, 2010
- ARS Maquette
  Angus R. Shamal, 1999, 2010
- Corporate S
  Kurt Weidemann, 1990
- Dagny
  Örjan Nordling, Göran Söderström, 2009
- Helvetica
  Max Miedinger with Edüard Hoffmann, 1957

Hand-embossed business cards feature
the Humanist serif typeface Centaur. Set
solely in tracked uppercase, the typeface
is elegant. Capitals are one of Centaur's
finest assets. Subtle changes in type
size, color, and value aid hierarchy.

———
PATRICK L CRAWFORD DESIGN

Old Style typeface Garamond pairs with Benton Sans (a contemporary revival of the 1903 Grotesque typeface News Gothic). Garamond conveys spirited messages framed in colorful talk bubbles. The letterforms are warm and friendly.

—

ADDIS CRESON

The Hartney logotype is set in Century Schoolbook, a Transitional serif typeface. Lowercase letterforms feature a tall x-height and open counters. The typeface personality is welcoming; a touch of italic adds sophistication. Geometric sans serif Futura in limited use complements the serif typeface.

—

NIEDERMEIER DESIGN

The iconic work for *Harper's Bazaar* by famed designer Alexey Brodovitch inspires the Anna McGregor logotype. The *A* is grand, typeset in the Modern serif Bauer Bodoni. The black and white palette reflects the extreme contrast inherent in the face.

—

NELSON ASSOCIATES

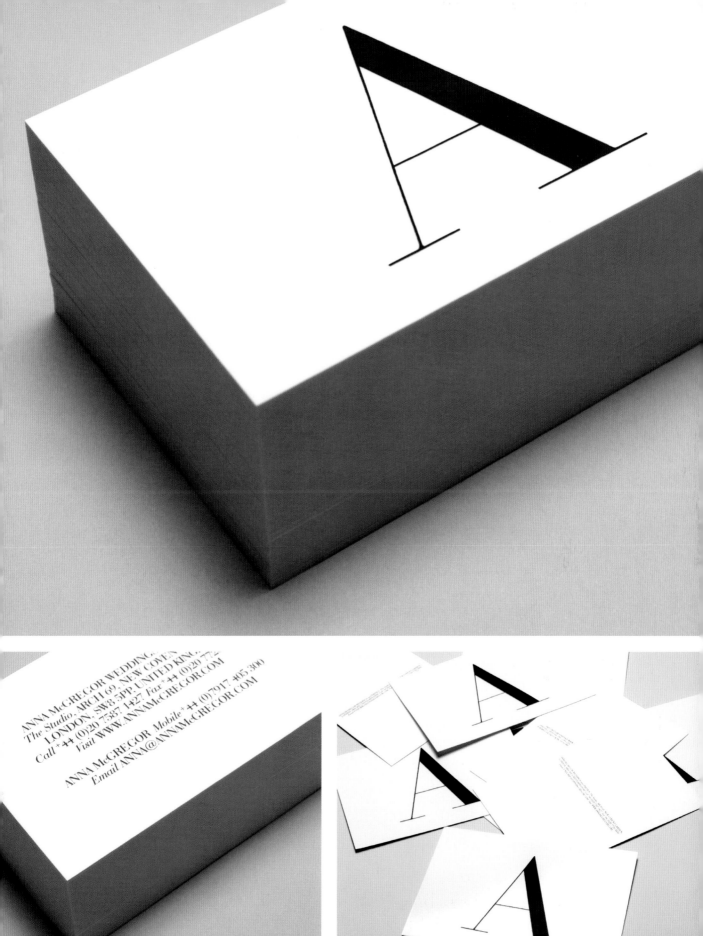

ANNA McGREGOR WEDDING
The Studio, MRCH 69 - NEW COVEN
LONDON, SW8 5PP. UNITED KING
Call + ++ (0)20 7587 1427 Fax + ++ (0)20 77
Visit WWW.ANNAMcGREGOR.COM
ANNA McGREGOR Mobile + ++ (07917 405 300
Email ANNA@ANNAMcGREGOR.COM

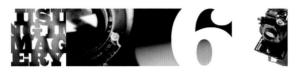

Web banners for an online course exhibit
strong figure-ground relationships. Slab
serif typefaces—Giza (an Egyptian slab)
with a pinch of Sentinel (a Clarendon slab)—
seamlessly interact with closely cropped
photographs. Letterforms, numerals, and
punctuation function as words, graphic
forms, and image carriers.

——
CHARLES GIBBONS

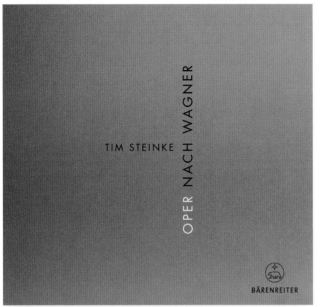

The photograph provides an implied vertical axis from which the book title *Oper Nach Wagner* rises. Title and author connect perpendicularly and echo the image. Orientation and type size variations order the text, set in Futura, the archetype of Geometric sans serifs.

—

TAKE OFF—MEDIA SERVICES

Grotesque sans serif Akzidenz-Grotesk grabs attention. Color identifies the band names—*Neat Neat Neat* and *The Dalles*—on the 7" (18 cm) record sleeve. Mixing with graphic elements and photography, type commands the design. Its scale and flush-left alignment give it a solid presence.

—

FALKO OHLMER

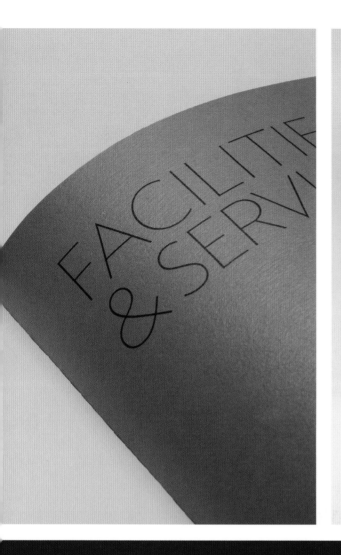

FACILITIES
& SERVICES

THE MAY FAIR

THE MAY FAIR

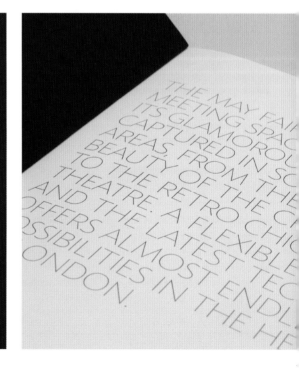

THE MAY FAIR
MEETING SPACE
ITS GLAMOROUS
CAPTURED IN SO
AREAS, FROM THE
BEAUTY OF THE C
TO THE RETRO CHIC
THEATRE. A FLEXIBLE
AND THE LATEST TEC
OFFERS ALMOST ENDL
POSSIBILITIES IN THE
LONDON.

Karen Cheng knows your type.

 TH.2\5\09
7P, RM.5401

Karen Cheng received her Master's Degree from the **University of Cincinnati College of Design**, Art, Architecture and Planning. Prior to joining the faculty at the University of Washington in 1997, she worked in Brand Management at the Procter and Gamble Company and studied engineering at Penn State University.

Her work has been published by *Communication Arts, the American Center for Design, Critique, the Society for Publication Designers, the University +College Designers Association, How Magazine* and *PIE Tokyo*.

She is active in the Seattle chapter of the AIGA, where she has been a board member and chair of the education committee. Her book, *Designing Type*, was published by Yale University Press in Spring 2006. She is currently Chair of the Visual Communication Design program.
*All UC students are invited to attend.

Classic Transitional sans serif Univers sits convincingly in a poster that promotes a lecture by designer, professor, and author Karen Cheng. Each line of the three-part title "Karen Cheng knows your type" changes weight from top to bottom—65 Bold to 55 Roman to 45 Light.

———

JESSE REED

The May Fair Hotel logotype is refined and contemporary. A redrawn version of the Humanist sans serif, Topaz has thin strokes that evoke timeless elegance. Collateral materials extend the logotype and capture the glamour and heritage of the London landmark.

———

NELSON ASSOCIATES

Typographer Beatrice Warde wrote: "There are bad types and good types, and the whole science and art of typography begins after the first category has been set aside."[2] What constitutes a good typeface? It is a system of thoughtfully conceived and constructed characters working together as words, lines, and paragraphs. It is highly legible, with well-considered space built in and around the characters. Good typefaces used with care and creativity serve texts, authors, and readers. Smart selections give designers the precise kit of parts to do this. However, everything is relative. Quality typefaces do not guarantee success—regardless of their legibility or attention to detail. A great face poorly handled still leaves text unreadable, just as ill-chosen typefaces send mixed messages. Conversely, fitting faces of mediocre merit work if typeset well. There are few absolutes. Like much in typography, flexible principles guide the process for choosing and combining typefaces.

To begin, start with the text—not the type. Take time to read and grasp it as well as possible. Get a sense of its mood and energy. Pinpoint the main message. Context initiates decision-making. Next, carefully map the text. Note its quantity and variety, or types of text, then order it by importance. Determine the technical needs of a typeface, such as stylistic range (posture, weight, and width) or special features (ligatures, numeral styles, and small caps), to create hierarchy. A project with limited types of text needs less typeface range than one with multiple variables. For example, books are textually rich, with many options such as body text, headings, captions, footers, and folios. When thinking about typefaces, begin with the text largest in quantity, most often body text. An ideal choice is a face designed for extended reading at small sizes in either serif or sans serif. In contrast, posters often contain minimal text, such as titles, dates, and brief descriptions. An attention-grabbing display face might echo the title perfectly, as a modest face conveys supporting text. Think first of the text and its typesetting needs, then make appropriate choices.

Typeface quality depends on character construction and how well the forms work together. This poster promotes the typeface Skolar, designed by David Březina. Skolar is a hearty text face with strong serifs and tall x-height, which aid reading at small sizes.

DAVID BŘEZINA

2 Beatrice Warde, "On the Choice of Typeface," in *Texts on Type: Critical Writings on Typography*, eds. Steven Heller and Philip B. Meggs (New York: Allworth Press, 2001), 196.

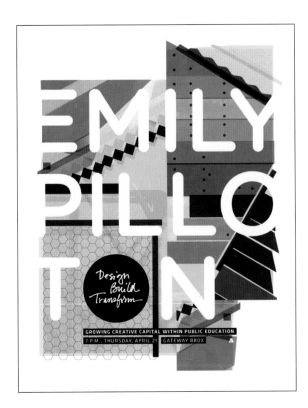

Determine the medium, users, and viewing conditions. Typefaces for environments observed from a distance vary greatly from tablets seen inches away. Those for corporate annual reports differ from children's books, as do the viewers. The former may lend itself to reserved typefaces set conservatively, the latter to friendly faces set expressively. Short-term assignments might require contemporary faces that speak to present-day social conditions. Trustworthy, classic characters might best assist long-term ventures. Innovative concepts can benefit from custom typefaces. Informed choices are essential. There are vast numbers of typefaces to discover (with many more to come). Regardless of the medium, seek excellent examples. Observing type in practice is a great way to learn.

The name Emily Pilloton set in Gotham Rounded knocks out of a graphic background in a poster promoting a lecture at the Maryland Institute College of Art. The face is friendly and contemporary. A second typeface, Klavika, contrasts Gotham. The sharp sans serif presents supporting text with clarity. A hand-lettered subtitle complements the typefaces.

AGGIE TOPPINS

The One Atlantic wine labels feature a custom typeface designed in collaboration with Darden Studio. It is distinctive and adds value. Letterforms demonstrate a posture shift from roman to oblique that marks the wine type. Color reinforces the typographic nuance.

MUCCA DESIGN

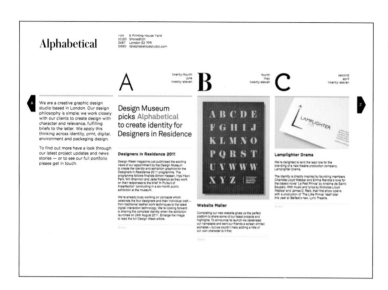

Particular media necessitate special consideration. Type for the web, as well as digital devices and gestural interfaces, meet challenges because conditions vary, unlike fixed mediums such as print. Multiple browsers, platforms, and screen sizes present type differently. Typefaces suited to one might not suit another. Expect the unexpected in digital realms. Be flexible and responsive. Digital formats know no bounds. Unlimited virtual space offers potential unseen in other areas. Digitally displayed, quality typography is progressing swiftly. For instance, web font technology advances at a rapid pace and makes available quality typefaces that work seamlessly on screen. Designers have options akin to fine print work minus the technical hurdles that once limited web and digital display type. Barriers across platforms and devices, as well as mediums, are minimized. Demand for and access to first-rate typographic settings (and the technical means to execute it) in digital mediums is growing. Such great typographic potential and invention exists!

Typefaces create atmosphere. They spark emotions and express historical, contemporary, or cultural connotations—all before the text is read. Subtle messaging via the physical characteristics of typefaces prompts viewer participation. Some faces are casual or dignified, others mechanical or playful. Univers is neutral and no-nonsense and can be dressed up or down. It looks good in everything. Robust and friendly Clarendon sits firmly without intimidation. Mrs Eaves charms; it is traditional with contemporary flair. A fitting typeface personality makes an impression.

An apt twenty-six typefaces add typographic character to the Alphabetical website. Letterforms from A to Z, each distinct, organize the site, which is a portfolio and news stream fusion. Support text, as seen in the contact information, dates, and headings, are set in Gotham.

—

ALPHABETICAL

æ fb ct fy ee ff gi fh ip fj ky fl gg gy oe sp ggy fr st ft ip py tw tt ty tty

N AA MB OC MD FF OG HE FI UB FL LA NT OO MP E U UD TT UP VA TW UL TY UR

Aa Bb Cc Dd Ee Ff Gg Hh Ii Jj Kk Ll Mm Nn Oo Pp Qq Rr Ss Tt Uu Vv Ww Xx Yy Zz
a b c d e f g h i j k l m n o p q r s t u v w x y z

AaBbCc1234

Aa Bb Cc Dd Ee Ff Gg Hh Ii Jj Kk Ll Mm Nn Oo Pp Qq Rr Ss Tt Uu Vv Ww Xx Yy Zz

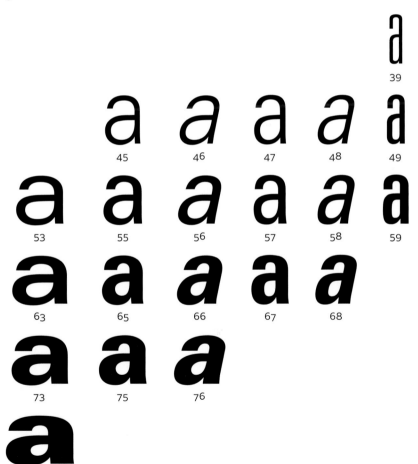

39
45 46 47 48 49
53 55 56 57 58 59
63 65 66 67 68
73 75 76
83

A A Baskerville revival, Zuzana Licko's Mrs Eaves is a serif typeface featuring open counters and supple curves. A notable feature is its extensive ligatures. Named after Sarah Eaves, John Baskerville's housekeeper and later wife, Mrs Eaves is stylish, charismatic, and gracious.

B Robert Besley created the original Clarendon in 1845. (In the 1900s, it was updated by Monotype and again later by Hermann Eidenbenz.) Its distinctive slab serifs make it stand out in display settings. Bracketed serifs and ball terminals contribute to its friendly, stout personality.

C Univers, designed by Adrian Frutiger in 1957, was the first typeface to use a numerical naming system for each font (the original design contained twenty-one fonts). The first number defines type weight, the second width. The typeface offers variety in a cohesive, legible package. Its neutral tone is an asset. Univers can wear many hats and satisfy diverse projects.

Aa

Display
24 point and up
48 pt Minion

Aa

Subhead
14 to 24 point
24 pt Minion

Aa

Body
9 to 14 point
14 pt Minion

Aa

Caption
6 to 8 point
8 pt Minion

Aa Aa Aa

Subhead, Body, Caption
L to R

Aa Aa Aa

Display, Body, Caption
L to R

Aa Aa Aa

Display, Subhead, Caption
L to R

Aa Aa Aa

Display, Subhead, Body
L to R

Examine the design of typefaces. Look for legible, well-proportioned, and acutely crafted characters. When typeset, words and lines read fluidly. Reliable typefaces have consistent styles (posture, weight, and width) to provide for typographic variation and emphasis. Depending on the quantity and variety of text, a range of styles—from light to bold weights and condensed to extended widths—add versatility. Likewise, ligatures, swash characters, and alternate glyphs offer diversity. Certain typefaces, including Minion by Robert Slimbach, have optical styles, commonly caption, body, subhead, and display. Optical styles feature subtle adjustments in letter-form contrast, proportion, and weight that enhance appearance at specific point sizes. For example, if setting type above 24 point, use the display style, which appears too thin at small sizes. Conversely, 6- to 8-point type size requires caption styles, which look too heavy at large sizes. Optical styles represent fine attention to detail. No matter the type size needed, optimal forms exist. Ample typefaces offer typographic opportunities.

Slight adjustments in contrast, proportion, and weight optimize typefaces used at specific point sizes. Caption and body styles designed for comfortable and extended reading perform well at small sizes. They are too dense and muddy enlarged. Subhead and display styles crafted to shine at large sizes fall short when they are reduced. Stroke quality is lost. Optical styles maintain typeface legibility and elegance at all sizes when used as planned.

In this student project, changes in point size and weight create variation and emphasis. The contrast is simple and effective with just one typeface—Helvetica. Confident type settings convey the Knoll brand.

—

KRISTÍN AGNARSDÓTTIR

Examine **letterform** anatomy.

a a *a* a

Sentinel and Whitney, Hoefler & Frere-Jones

Compare *and* contrast *features*.

Epic, Neil Summerour
Alright Sans, Jackson Cavanaugh

Seek the typefaces *of one designer*, as they often share **approach** and **style**.

Glypha and Univers, Adrian Frutiger

Science does not apply when it comes to pairing typefaces. Examine letterform anatomy. Compare and contrast features. Seek the typefaces of one designer—they often have a similar approach and style. Let intuition lead decision-making. What looks optically fit is often good. Strive for distinction that suits the content.

Starting out, begin with one quality typeface. A dependable choice normally meets all needs. For instance, proven effective over time, Helvetica by Max Miedinger is ever-present. Sometimes one typeface is not enough. Creating broader typeface palettes has benefits. Multiple faces differentiate types of text. They extend typesetting possibilities and foster rich typographic color and texture. Relationships between typefaces, typically up to two or three, deepen personality. In all cases, thoughtful deliberation leads the way.

Pairing one serif and sans serif typeface works in most situations. Contrast is key. Check comparative and contrasting features, such as letterform proportion, x-height, stroke quality, and stress. Typefaces with similar x-heights and counters mix nicely. Specific letterforms also provide cues. Look for consistent anatomy traits. For example, typefaces with double story characters (lowercase *a* and *g*) might pair better than one face with them, the other without. Examine all typeface offerings. If text calls for small caps and multiple numeral sets, choose faces that include them. Avoid redundancy. Typefaces with marked likeness, such as those from the same category, are poorly matched partners.

In use, assign each typeface specific roles. For instance, body text may look best set in a highly legible serif face designed for reading. A complementary sans serif serves brief captions or subheads well. Text in limited quantity, such as title pages or short headings, works nicely in striking display faces. When combining typefaces, carefully review the size relationships between letterforms. Match them optically, not by point size. At the same size, one typeface can look larger or smaller than another when set side by side. Subtle adjustments create balanced combinations. Be decisive. Use typeface combinations to enrich and clarify text.

Too similar angled crossbars on the lowercase *e*
Centaur and Jenson

Too similar hairline, unbracketed serifs
Bodoni and Walbaum

Too similar stroke contrast and counters
Frutiger and Myriad

Typefaces of the same category make unhappy companions. When mixing typefaces, distinction between them is vital. Contrast loses to similarity. Competing identities do not benefit the text they aim to distinguish.

The One Love Organics packaging typography is fresh and elegant. Serif Filosofia and san serif Gotham are the dominant typefaces. The designer's lettering (with a color splash) marks the products' names. Handwriting combines with the type and adds a human touch.

———

ONE LOVE ORGANICS

Bodoni and Univers unite in identity
materials and menus for the New York
City restaurant and cocktail bar Compose.
Bodoni directs the eye to names, menu
items, and prices. Its poised setting
emphasizes the typeface attributes
of high stroke contrast and majestic
majuscules. Descriptive text set in
Univers supports the refined serif.

———

JESSE REED

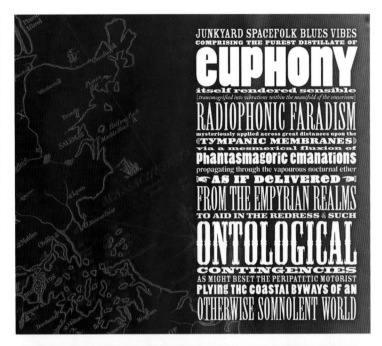

The book series *Temas de Psicanálise* (*Themes of Psychoanalysis*) uses Century Schoolbook and Scala Sans on the spines. The typefaces distinguish titles from authors with the support of type size and case changes.

———

FBA.

Ten typefaces appear on the CD cover *Moonmonster* (one in a series called *The Book of a Number of Hours*). The mix, which includes Giza, Zapata, and Ironmonger, is striking. Typographic expertise is required to manage this combination and quantity of faces. The back cover quietly contrasts the front with one typeface, Historical Fell.

———

CHARLES GIBBONS

DISPLAY	BIG	TEXT	MICRO	SANS
a *a* A A	a *a* A A	a *a* A A	a *a* A A	a a A A
LIGHT	LIGHT	LIGHT	LIGHT	LIGHT
a *a* A A	a *a* A A	a *a* A A	a *a* A A	a a A A
BOOK	BOOK	BOOK	BOOK	BOOK
a *a* A A	a *a* A A	a *a* A A	a *a* A A	a a A A
MEDIUM	MEDIUM	MEDIUM	MEDIUM	MEDIUM
a *a* A A	a *a* A A	a *a* A A	a *a* A A	a a A A
SEMIBOLD	SEMIBOLD	SEMIBOLD	SEMIBOLD	SEMIBOLD
a *a* A A	a *a* A A	a *a* A A	a *a* A A	a a A A
BOLD	BOLD	BOLD	BOLD	BOLD
a *a* A A	a *a* A A	a *a* A A	a *a* A A	a a A A
BLACK	BLACK	BLACK	BLACK	BLACK

—

JOSHUA DARDEN

If seeking multiple typefaces, superfamilies are excellent choices. Designed as full-bodied typographic systems, they offer consistency across serif, semi serif, sans serif, semi sans, and slab serif typefaces. Whether using two, three, or four faces, superfamilies harmonize. One size fits all.

Sans Serif
Sans Serif Italic
Sans Serif Bold
Sans Serif Bold Italic
Mix
Mix Italic
Mix Bold
Mix Bold Italic
Serif
Serif Italic
Serif Bold
Serif Bold Italic

Nexus

—

MARTIN MAJOOR

Sans Serif
Sans Serif Italic
Sans Serif Bold
Sans Serif Extra Bold
Semi Sans Light
Semi Sans Light Italic
Semi Sans
Semi Sans Italic
Semi Sans Bold
Semi Sans Extra Bold
Semi Serif
Semi Serif Bold
Sans Serif Light
Sans Serif Light Italic
Serif
Serif Italic
Serif Bold

Rotis

—

OTL AICHER

Superfamilies simplify the process of combining typefaces. They may include serif, semi serif, sans serif, semi sans, and slab serif faces. Extensive weights and widths, as well as optical styles, are common. Unified by concept and form, superfamilies add unique flavor to typographic works, all connected by family ties. For instance, type designer Martin Majoor's Nexus ("connection" in Latin) contains serif, sans serif, and slab serif typefaces. He describes it as "three typefaces, one form principle."[3] The allied and versatile threesome stems from one design concept driving its development. (A monospaced typewriter face adds character to the core trio.) A second example is Rotis by Otl Aicher, which contains serif, semi serif, sans, and semi sans faces. Used interchangeably, the typefaces transition effortlessly from one to the next. Superfamilies are comprehensive systems fit for wide-ranging, particularly complex, typographic projects.

An abundance of typefaces exists. Although a handful can be enough to last a lifetime, explore and test faces of all sorts. Create specimens with a range of settings suited to specific texts and mediums. No matter the situation, always review typefaces in context. For instance, print samples. What looks great on screen might not translate on paper. Review typefaces in multiple browsers and screen resolutions, as well as digital devices. Mock up three-dimensional environments or packages. Know what type looks like in specific mediums. Tailor aptly. Good typefaces fittingly selected—and expressed with skilled treatment— yield beautiful results.

3 "FF Nexus," *FontFont Focus,*
  FSI FontShop International, 2007.

4

TYPESETTING
FACTORS

"TYPOGRAPHIC STYLE,

in this large and intelligent sense of the word, does not mean any particular style—

my style or your style, or neoclassical or baroque style—but the power to move

freely through the whole domain of typography, and to function at every step

in a way that is graceful and vital instead of banal. It means typography that can

walk familiar ground without sliding into platitudes, typography that responds

to new conditions with innovative solutions, and typography that does not

vex the reader with its own originality in a self-conscious search for praise."

from The Elements of Typographic Style

ROBERT BRINGHURST

Intelligent treatments and attention to detail are emphases of typographic craft. Transforming text with type that articulates it well rests with designers. Typesetting principals lead the way. Learned methods of typographic handling become second nature with repetition. Proceed with care. Principles and access to typographic tools and software do not always render effective results. Set type convincingly through decisive use—avoid relying solely on principles. Adaptable thinking is essential. Applying principles well is equal to reworking or discarding them for best results. Setting type also relies heavily on optical, not mechanical, factors (or default settings). What looks correct visually most often stands— a challenging concept to convey, especially to beginners. Typographic training involves learning to see with keen eyes. Observing type critically, notably flaws that inhibit function, offers valued insight to set it well. Detect problems (unseen by most) and fix them. Ensure nothing comes between the words and the readers. Skilled type-setting involves learned principles and practice plus thoughtful observation and treatment.

Author name and book title typeset in TheSans (from the superfamily Thesis) on the cover of the book, *Handle. Die Opern*, share size and weight. Color and position shifts distinguish them. The photograph inspires the color choices, which ties type and image together.

———

TAKE OFF—MEDIA SERVICES

Serif Mercury and sans serif Knockout combine on the *International Drawing Annual* cover. Three levels of text— organization name, tagline, and book title— share uppercase settings and justified alignments. Changes in type size, width, and tracking provide variation.

———

AUGUST BUREAU

SELECTED READINGS

Explorations in Typography:
Mastering the Art of Fine Typesetting
Carolina de Bartolo
with Erik Spiekermann

Typography: Macro + Microaesthetics
Willi Kunz

TYPOGRAPHIC COLOR

Typographic color refers to overall type lightness and darkness based on value, not on hue. Light and dark values influence type appearance and hierarchy. Type lacking color is dull and flat; strong color enlivens works with variation and emphasis. Text quantity, typeface, and space in and around letterforms combined with well-articulated factors such as type size, style, and spacing shape typographic color. Dark elements make strong imprints; light elements connote openness. Their interaction nurtures spatial depth, rhythm, and texture—all highly desirable typesetting attributes.

In *Typography: A Manual of Design*, designer and typographer Emil Ruder writes: "The oriental philosophers hold that the essence of created form depends on empty space. Without its hollow interior a jug is merely a lump of clay, and it is only the empty space inside that makes it into a vessel." Typesetting happens in accord with the space in and around it. Space is as much a physical presence as typographic marks. Their collective relationship enlivens works. Space can change the look and feel of type, noticeably improving or weakening it. The act of spacing adjusts and refines the distances between characters, as well as the overall appearance of words, lines, and paragraphs. It includes kerning, tracking, and leading (line spacing). The terms *normal*, *loose*, *tight*, and *negative* describe spacing. *Normal* typically means an even, gray field of text. It lacks light and dark values, called typographic color (not hue), which vary and emphasize. For instance, tight spacing creates a blacker impression than loosely spaced type. Readability declines as spacing decreases or increases beyond average ranges: type looks awkwardly squeezed or scattered. Key spacing goals are balance and consistency. The eye guides because spacing type relies on optical sensitivity. What works well once might not work again; always space with a delicate touch, case by case.

DADA | THE BEGINNING

Because of Switzerland's famed policy of political neutrality, Zurich served as a safe haven for those escaping the escalating conflagration of World War I. Iconoclasts of all kinds were attracted to the city: pacifists, draft dodgers, spies, and profiteers, as well as political and intellectual refugees of many stripes, including the Russian Bolshevik exiles Vladimir Lenin and Grigori Zinoviev and the anarchist Mikhail Bakunin. In relation to Berlin, Munich, Bucharest, and Paris, where the founding dadaists had spent their pre-war years, Zurich was by all accounts a conservative city. Its very tranquility, abundance, and disengagement from the conflict created at times a feeling of unreal isolation from the larger European world. At one point in his memoirs, Richard Huelsenbeck, a founding member of the Zurich Dada group, writing with cosmopolitan disdain, labeled the entire country **"one big sanatorium."** But Huelsenbeck also clearly conveyed the overarching sense of freedom and relief that accompanied his arrival in Zurich: **"In the liberal atmosphere of Zurich, where the newspapers could print what they pleased, where there were no ration stamps and no 'ersatz' food, we could scream out everything we were bursting with."** This sense of refuge was shadowed by a keen awareness of proximity to threat, felt both geographically and physically. Hans Arp wrote defiantly: **"Despite the remote booming of artillery, we sang, painted, pasted and wrote poetry with all our might,"** while Hugo Ball drew a more precarious picture, describing Switzerland as a **"birdcage, surrounded by roaring lions."**

The origins of the Dada movement are inextricably tied to the short life of the Cabaret Voltaire, an iconoclastic nightclub that served as the first public gathering place for Dada artists and writers. The learned Ball, the Cabaret's founder with his companion Emmy Hennings, served as

1   Richard Huelsenbeck, MEMOIRS OF DADA DRUMMER (1969), ed. Hans J. Kleinschmidt, trans. Joachim Neugroschel (Berkeley, 1991), 25.

2   Huelsenbeck, DADA DRUMMER, 14.

In this student project, text is ordered using typographic color, position, and variation of line spacing and type styles. Open leading in the first paragraph gives notice distinct from others. It is light in typographic color. Quotes in body text achieve strong contrast through weight and width changes from Univers 55 Regular to 67 Condensed Bold. The method allows the text to be easily scanned. Footnotes are consistently positioned below the body text with captions on verso pages. Repeated settings and positions of key elements aid typographic hierarchy and navigation.

———

AKSHATA WADEKAR

The regional charter publication, *Het Streekpact Voor de Westhoek* (*The Regional Pact in Flanders Fields*), offers an example of apt tracking applied to uppercase settings (in the typeface Trajan), which rely on open spacing for best recognition.

———

DESIGN SENSE

Kerning adjusts slight spaces between characters and corrects ill-fitting pairs that distract because of collisions or gaps. Certain combinations appear too close to or far from each other when typeset by default. Such pairs are common with letterforms that combine with *T*, *V*, *W*, and *Y*—for example *Ty*, *Va*, *Wi*, and *Ye*. Numerals, notably *1*, often need kerning to bring others closer to or farther from them. Slivers of space around punctuation like em dashes (—) and backslashes (/) set well with attentive tunings. A well-designed typeface has considered kerning pairs, which ease typesetting because quality spacing is inherent. Still, regardless of the typeface strength, manual adjustments can be required. Body (9 to 14 point) and caption (6 to 8 point) styles typically need less notice than display styles (24 point and up) because space between characters grows at large type sizes. Irregularities are more evident. Kerning fixes awkward appearances.

Tracking affects the overall spacing of words, lines, and paragraphs. Normal tracking refers to standard spacing set by default without adjustments. Type designers preset it in typefaces. When used decisively, tracking improves type appearance. For instance, uppercase settings (full and small caps) rely on open tracking for identification. Their lack of ascenders and descenders slows readability. Added space around such characters improves recognition. The same applies to sequences of lining figures (numerals the same height as uppercase letterforms), such as phone numbers and zip codes. Alternatively, lowercase settings typically need less tracking because ascenders and descenders improve identification. Condensed typefaces with narrow proportions and counters in upper and lowercase may benefit from slightly open tracking. Avoid tracking paragraphs or continuous text. When spaced too loosely, tightly, or negatively, paragraphs no longer read fluidly.

Kerning

TRACKING

Typography

Irregular Spacing

Typography

Adjusted Spacing

1950–2012

Irregular Spacing

1950–2012

Adjusted Spacing

UPPERCASE

Before Tracking

UPPERCASE

After Tracking

lowercase

Normal Spacing

l o w e r c a s e

Too Loose Spacing

lowercase

Too Tight Spacing

Kerning

Attentive typesetting will eliminate unwanted collisions or gaps that distract. Kerning adjusts the slivers of space between characters. Such fixes are common with letterforms next to *T*, *V*, *W*, and *Y*. Delicate shifts closer to or farther from one another remedy awkward character combinations. Numerals, especially those paired with *1*, often require care, as do punctuation marks, including dashes, parentheses, and backslashes. Character space increases at large type sizes and makes errors more apparent. Kerning finesses type for best presentation.

Tracking

Tracking affects overall spacing of words, lines, and paragraphs to enhance readability. Uppercase settings (full and small caps) and lining numeral sequences rely on open tracking for recognition. Lowercase settings typically need little to no tracking because of their variation in shape. Condensed typefaces with narrow proportions and counters in upper and lowercase can often benefit from slight tracking. Avoid tracking paragraphs or continuous text. Words, lines, and paragraphs loosely, tightly, or negatively tracked look spotty and no longer read as intended.

"No matter how admirably we plan our work or how fine

in design are the types we select, its appearance when

printed depends on good composition—the combination

of type into words, the arrangement of words into lines,

and the assemblage of lines to make pages."

Positive Leading 9/24

"No matter how admirably we plan our work or how fine
in design are the types we select, its appearance when
printed depends on good composition—the combination
of type into words, the arrangement of words into lines,
and the assemblage of lines to make pages."

Solid Leading 9/9

"No matter how admirably we plan our work or how fine
in design are the types we select, its appearance when
printed depends on good composition—the combination
of type into words, the arrangement of words into lines,
and the assemblage of lines to make pages."

Negative Leading 9/6

"No matter how admirably we plan our work
                    Typographers on Type:
or how fine in design are the types we select,
                    An Illustrated Anthology from
its appearance when printed depends on good
                    William Morris to the Present Day
composition—the combination of type into
                    Ruari McLean, ed.
words, the arrangement of words into lines,
                    W. W. Norton
and the assemblage of lines to make pages."

Overlapping Leading 9/24

Leading is the vertical distance from one baseline to the next measured in points. Leading options are positive, negative, and solid. Positive leading is greater than the point size; negative leading is less. Solid leading equals point size. Positive leading is apt for most type settings. Negative leading can work for display styles (24 point and up) but not body styles (9 to 14 point). Leading depth varies and is influenced by type size, x-height, and line length. Start with leading that is at least larger than word spaces. Examine ascent (the maximum letterform height from the baseline beyond the cap line) and descent (the maximum letterform distance below the baseline). Typefaces with tall ascenders and long descenders require more line spacing to avoid touching. Long versus short lines also need open leading because the eye travels farther from one line to another. Too much paragraph leading creates loose interline space. It gives the appearance of single lines, not sequential thoughts. Tight leading shapes compact text blocks, which can be difficult to navigate because of the limited space between lines. Viewers see too much at once. Leading can also overlap, which weaves together lines of type. One text fits into the line space of another. Overlapping leading offers visual interest, as well as typographic texture, via merged yet contrasting text.

Leading is the vertical distance from one baseline to the next measured in points. It is positive, negative, or solid. Positive leading is greater than the type size, solid leading equal to it. Negative leading is less than the type size such as 9-point type size with 6-point leading. Overlapping leading is an alternate line spacing method that nests contrasting text types.

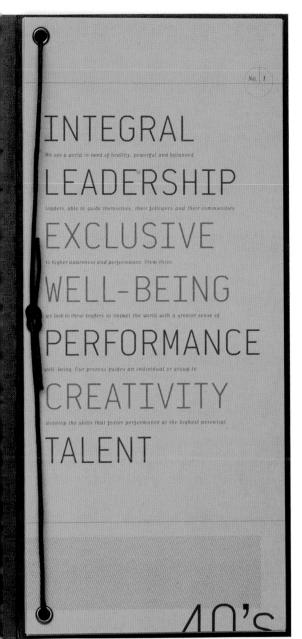

INTEGRAL

We see a world in need of healthy, powerful and balanced

LEADERSHIP

leaders, able to guide themselves, their followers, and their communities

EXCLUSIVE

to higher awareness and performance. From there,

WELL-BEING

we look to these leaders to impact the world with a greater sense of

PERFORMANCE

well-being. Our process guides an individual or group to

CREATIVITY

develop the skills that foster performance at the highest potential.

TALENT

40's

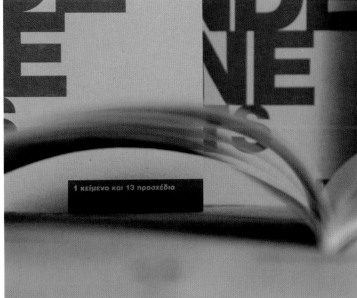

Overlapping leading is an alternate line spacing method that intermixes different text. One text fits into the line space of another. It nests without distraction and adds typographic texture. Combined typefaces, Deck and Matrix, as well as type size, distinguish content.

———
BLOK DESIGN

The exhibition catalog and invitation details for the Vakalo School of Art and Design (Athens, Greece) illustrate solid leading, in which the leading equals type size. Baselines of uppercase letterforms in the typeface Helvetica stack on cap lines for a bold impression.

———
DESPINA AERAKI
GIOTA KOKKOSI

By 1999, worldwide hemp retail receipts were estimated at $150,000,000 with the *United States'* consumer purchasing over 60% of that amount. These numbers do not take into account the large quantities absorbed by commercial and industrial users in the U.S. and around the world, whose major purchases have justified the planting of tens of thousands of acres in 31 other countries.

Had it been legal to harvest *industrial hemp* in the U.S., our economy would have seen a growth of approximately $90,000,000 instead of fueling that of other countries.

Learn the facts about Industrial Hemp and the lucrative impact our country can gain from harvesting this crop.

Be Informed. *Vote Hemp.* www.HempAmerica.com

HEMP AMERICA

Typographic alignment refers to type configurations. Alignments are flush-left/ragged right (FL, FL/RR); flush-right/ragged left (FR, FR/RL); centered (C); and justified (J). Flush-left settings are common and offer reading ease because the starting points of lines and paragraphs are fixed. They nurture left to right reading with comfort. Flush-right alignments are fit for words or lines. They contrast well with flush-left text, when juxtaposed along alignment edges. A ragged left edge creates irregular starting points per line, which can make reading paragraphs difficult. Centered alignments connote formality and classic typography. Useful in limited settings with minimal text, such as book title pages, centering rarely applies to continuous text (running paragraphs). Justified settings create clean lines and strong left and right alignment edges. Justified paragraphs pose challenges when variable word spaces, which flex in width based on type size and line-length relationships, cause noticeable flaws such as rivers (unsightly gaps or holes that appear in justified settings).

A call-to-action poster promotes the benefits of industrial hemp. A flush-left headline in DIN commands notice. Body text set in Newzald adopts the same alignment. The paragraph features a subtle rag with light in-and-out movement along the ragged right edge. Graphic carriers emphasize select text.

———

JESSE REED

Paragraphs are the largest text bodies in typographic design. Optimal settings seek balance among type size, line length, and leading. Type size is neither too small nor big. Line length is neither too narrow nor wide. Leading is neither too tight nor open. Forty-five to seventy-five characters per line is an ideal range for continuous text. A line length that is too wide makes it difficult to travel back across the paragraph to the next line and is tiring to read. Small type sizes are often ill-suited to long lines; there are too many words per line. If the line length is too short, the transition to the next line happens too quickly, and disjointed reading arises. Large type sizes fit poorly in narrow line lengths because the word count per line is limited, and excessive hyphenation, which is typically best prevented, may occur. Generous leading may break paragraphs into individual lines rather than sequential thoughts. Tight, solid, or negative leading merges lines together. Either too much is read at once or lines collide. Avoid forcing paragraphs into unsuitable arrangements. Uphold continuous text integrity and invite readers into paragraphs with considered treatments.

Line length describes the width of a text line, measured in picas. An ideal line length contains forty-five to seventy-five characters per line. If too long, it is difficult to move across and down to the next line. If too short, the transition to the next line happens too quickly. Large type sizes work best with wide line lengths, small type with narrow.

Forty-five to seventy-five characters per line is an ideal range for continuous text. A line length that is too wide makes it difficult to travel back across the paragraph to the next line and is tiring to read. Small type sizes are often ill-suited to long lines; there are too many words per line. If the line length is too short, the transition to the next line happens too quickly, and disjointed reading arises. Large type sizes fit poorly in narrow line lengths because the word count per line is limited, and excessive hyphenation, which is typically best prevented, may occur.

Above Average Line Length
89 characters per line

Optimal settings seek balance among type size, line length, and leading. Forty-five to seventy-five characters per line is an ideal range for continuous text.

Average Line Length
68 characters per line

Forty-five to seventy-five characters per line is an ideal range for continuous text. A line length that is too wide makes it difficult to travel back across the paragraph to the next line and is tiring to read. Small type sizes are often ill-suited to long lines; there are too many words per line. If the line length is too short, the transition to the next line happens too quickly, and disjointed reading arises. Large type sizes fit poorly in narrow line lengths because the word count per line is limited, and excessive hyphenation, which is typically best prevented, may occur.

Below Average Line Length
31 characters per line

Forty-five to seventy-five characters per line is an ideal range for continuous text. A line length that is too wide makes it difficult to travel back across the paragraph to the next line and is tiring to read. Small type sizes are often ill-suited to long lines; there are too many words per line. If the line length is too short, the transition to the next line happens too quickly, and disjointed reading arises. Large type sizes fit poorly in narrow line lengths because the word count per line is limited, and excessive hyphenation, which is typically best prevented, may occur.

Average Line Length
45 characters per line

Designers engage with words, typographically expressing them with purpose and poise. Typography is a process, a refined craft making language visible. Designers shape language with type and give words life and power to speak text fluently. Letterforms and their supporting characters are simple shapes that do so much. With distinct voices and personalities, type whispers delicately and shouts loudly. Communication lies at its core. Type is commanding and beautiful one moment, analytic and instructive the next. It is dramatic, whimsical, modest, and extravagant. Typographic practice (and those dedicated to it) gives spoken and written language vitality across time, generations, and cultures.

Designers engage with words, typographically expressing them with purpose and poise. Typography is a process, a refined craft making language visible. Designers shape language with type and give words life and power to speak text fluently. Letterforms and their supporting characters are simple shapes that do so much. With distinct voices and personalities, type whispers delicately and shouts loudly. Communication lies at its core. Type is commanding and beautiful one moment, analytic and instructive the next. It is dramatic, whimsical, modest, and extravagant. Typographic practice (and those dedicated to it) gives spoken and written language vitality across time, generations, and cultures.

Flush Right FR, FR/RL
Flush-right alignments are best suited to words or lines, rather than paragraphs. Flush right contrasts well with flush left text, when juxtaposed along alignment edges. Flush right is less fitting for paragraphs because the start of each line varies in position. The stable left edge seen in flush-left and justified alignments fosters improved reading conditions for continuous text.

Flush Left FL, FL/RR
Flush left is a multipurpose alignment method, especially for paragraphs. It offers a fixed point from which words, lines, and paragraphs begin, which eases left to right reading. Fixed word space typically makes ragging easier to manage than justified alignments with variable word space.

Designers engage with words, typographically expressing them with purpose and poise. Typography is a process, a refined craft making language visible. Designers shape language with type and give words life and power to speak text fluently. Letterforms and their supporting characters are simple shapes that do so much. With distinct voices and personalities, type whispers delicately and shouts loudly. Communication lies at its core. Type is commanding and beautiful one moment, analytic and instructive the next. It is dramatic, whimsical, modest, and extravagant. Typographic practice (and those dedicated to it) gives spoken and written language vitality across time, generations, and cultures.

Designers engage with words, typographically expressing them with purpose and poise. Typography is a process, a refined craft making language visible. Designers shape language with type and give words life and power to speak text fluently. Letterforms and their supporting characters are simple shapes that do so much. With distinct voices and personalities, type whispers delicately and shouts loudly. Communication lies at its core. Type is commanding and beautiful one moment, analytic and instructive the next. It is dramatic, whimsical, modest, and extravagant. Typographic practice (and those dedicated to it) gives spoken and written language vitality across time, generations, and cultures.

Centered C
Centered alignments fit short amounts of text, such as that in title pages, packaging, or business cards. Centering is rarely practical for running paragraphs. Left and right ragged lines do not offer alignment points for support text, nor do they create relationships with format edges.

Justified J
Justified alignment often produces harder, geometric settings with clean flush edges. It has variable word spaces, which means word spaces flex in width, based on type size, line length, and number of characters per line. Attention to such factors is vital to well-justified settings, which are prone to rivers—disruptive gaps and holes that run through justified paragraphs.

Spreads from the Realm Charter School brochure display flush-left and -right alignments. Flush-right settings work well in limited cases, such as single lines, as seen here. Consistent positioning along the top and side format edges, as well as type set in Nexus Mix (from the superfamily Nexus), offer unity. Support text at spread bottoms set flush left in the typefaces Nexus Typewriter and Vitesse share information about students' daily activities.

———
MINE™

A handbill with limited text is best set in a centered alignment. The piece announces a musical event at The Monastery Manchester. Combined typefaces, including Trade Gothic, Blackoak, Campanile, Freebooter Script, JF Ferrule, Stymie, and Clarendon convey a sense of Victorian Age printed matter.

———

IMAGINE-CGA

Centered alignments express formality and tradition. Business cards for the wealth management company Florin Kildare aptly reflect such qualities. Customized type settings (the logotype is a redrawn version of Austin with text in Monotype Baskerville) and premium-handcrafted papers convey confidence, heritage, and trustworthiness.

———

NELSON ASSOCIATES

Justified body text with ample line length offers a clean edge for footnotes stemming off it in a flush-left alignment. Serif typeface Utopia in different type sizes further distinguishes text in an exhibition catalog that celebrates Portuguese literature. An uppercase treatment plus color shift introduces opening words of the first paragraph with distinction.

—

FBA.

Dense fields of justified type in the sans serif Knockout grab attention on the Grip Limited website. Type size varies per line to best fit measures and maintain consistent tracking. Slab serif Archer delicately complements Knockout in limited type settings such as "Contact Us," "About Us," and "Jobs." Multiple navigation options support collapsible columns and ensure the design is user friendly.

GRIP LIMITED

A paragraph indicator is a visual cue that signals the beginning of a new thought. It is a silent note that provides a fleeting pause and smooth transition from one paragraph to another. Reading continues fluidly and does not halt.

Multiple methods exist to signal new paragraphs. Common paragraph indicators are indents and half or full line returns. A traditional indent is equivalent to one em space. Exaggerated indents range up to half the measure of the line length. Outdents are expressive indicators. First lines of paragraphs shift outside the body text, rather than into it. Length varies, depending on the desired effect. Graphic elements such as circles or squares, and symbols such as fleurons (❦), fists (☞), or pilcrows (paragraph sign)(¶) are other paragraph indicators. Such devices can be lighter in color or value than body text. Be inventive, but be careful not to over-indicate paragraphs—it can inhibit reading and result in the indicator being more prominent than the text.

Opening paragraphs, such as chapter or section introductions, are starting points, not continuations. Thus, paragraph indicators that signal a change from the preceding paragraphs are not needed. First lines of beginning paragraphs occasionally merit special attention, such as typographic variation. Investigate changes in type size, style, or case. Try a baseline shift, which is a type position change above or below the baseline. A companion typeface is also effective. Drop caps add ornate flair when fit to content. Opening lines and paragraphs are invitations to readers. Create a unique start when appropriate. Establish a fitting tone for paragraphs that follow.

Indent
A traditional approach is an indent equivalent to one em space. Indents can also match the leading. Be sure that they are not too slight, which can look like an extra space or unplanned misstep. An indent alternative equals half the paragraph measure or line length. Such extension might be excessive for large amounts of continuous text, but in limited use, the exaggerated effect is unexpected and dramatic.

Full and Half Line Returns
Full and half line returns signal breaks between paragraphs. A full line return maintains baseline alignment (see chapter 5), if in place. Full returns can benefit paragraphs with leading of little depth. The space between paragraphs is apparent; the pause is clear. Full returns applied to openly leaded paragraphs can distract. Too great a distance between paragraphs breaks them apart; the space is too large and leaves paragraphs in chunks. Sequential thought ceases. A half line return is a reasonable substitute. It is any measure greater than the leading but less than a full return. Tailor appropriately.

Outdent

An outdent refers to first lines that shift outside the paragraph body. Ledge-like in appearance, outdent lengths vary from a half to a full paragraph width or more. Outdents work well when dramatic effect is desired. They sometimes have a second emphasis factor, such as a style or case change, that contrasts with the body text.

Graphic Elements and Symbols

Graphic elements, such as circles, squares, and triangles, offer expressive ways to indicate paragraphs. Integrated throughout body text, they shape what looks like one paragraph. These devices often appear lighter in color or value than the body text. Embellished symbols, including fleurons (❦) or fists (☞), add decorative character. Consider the pilcrow (¶) for literal representation. Graphic elements and symbols require discretion to avoid being stronger than the paragraphs they signal.

■ A traditional approach is an indent equivalent to one em space. Indents can also match the leading. Be sure that they are not too slight, which can look like an extra space or unplanned misstep.

███████ An indent alternative equals half the paragraph measure or line length. Such extension might be excessive for large amounts of continuous text, but in limited use, the exaggerated effect is unexpected and dramatic.

Full and half line returns signal breaks between paragraphs. A full line return maintains baseline alignment, if in place.

24 POINT

Full returns can benefit paragraphs with leading of little depth. The space between paragraphs is apparent; the pause is clear. Full returns applied to openly leaded paragraphs can distract. Too great a distance between paragraphs breaks them apart; the space is too large and leaves paragraphs in chunks. Sequential thought ceases.

18 POINT

A half line return is a reasonable substitute. It is any measure greater than the leading but less than a full return. Tailor appropriately.

12-point Leading

OUTDENTS *refer to first lines that shift outside the paragraph body.* Ledge-like in appearance, outdent lengths vary from a half to a full paragraph width or more. Outdents work well when dramatic effect is desired. They sometimes have a second emphasis factor, such as a style or case change, that contrasts with the body text.

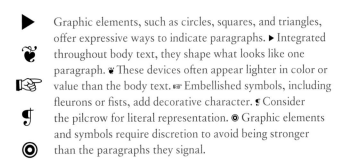

Graphic elements, such as circles, squares, and triangles, offer expressive ways to indicate paragraphs. ▶ Integrated throughout body text, they shape what looks like one paragraph. ❦ These devices often appear lighter in color or value than the body text. ☞ Embellished symbols, including fleurons or fists, add decorative character. ¶ Consider the pilcrow for literal representation. ◉ Graphic elements and symbols require discretion to avoid being stronger than the paragraphs they signal.

Ragging and hyphenation are methods that finesse paragraphs. Ragging is dedicated to fine-tuning paragraph edges with manual line breaks. It remedies line ends with awkward angles, curves, holes, and shapes that appear when using default settings. Rags may be active, with ample in-and-out movement from line to line, or understated, with subtle shifts. No absolute method exists. Achieve a smooth ebb and flow, and adjust anything that distracts from reading. Whether loose or tight, rag consistently. Prevent empty spaces, truncated words, short lines, or ledges that extend into or beyond the average line length. Discreet adjustments in column width or type size can assist ragging. Use such techniques in limited cases when manual line returns, hyphenation, or occasional copy edits do not solve the issues. Avoid ragging by tracking or manipulating word space. It often leads to inconsistent spacing. Save ragging until the end of typesetting with final text placed.

Typesetting without hyphenation is ideal but not realistic, especially for continuous text (running paragraphs). Hyphenation splits words across lines and improves typographic appearance. With it come many guidelines. Watch consecutive hyphenations at line ends—strive for no more than two in a row. Do not hyphenate proper names and nouns. The first and last full paragraph lines are hyphen free. Break words into grammatically correct syllables. Avoid hyphenating words with fewer than five letterforms. Split words down the middle in best cases. Too little left behind or brought ahead is awkward, for example, the –*ed* in "hyphenated." A rule of thumb is two letterforms behind, three ahead.

Rivers, orphans, and widows are further factors to control when refining paragraphs. Rivers are gaps or disruptive holes that run down and across justified alignments. Widows are one, two, or three short words on the last paragraph line. They do not fill enough line length; their diminutive stature draws attention. Review and alter previous lines with effort to add heft to the last line. It need not meet average line ends; half the measure is fitting. Orphans arise in multiple-page projects. They are first paragraph lines ending pages or last paragraph lines beginning new ones.

Hyphenation on line 1

Three hyphens in a row, lines 1, 2, and 3

Large hole, line 4

Angle, lines 4, 5, and 6

Ledge on line 9

Ragging and hyphenation are methods that finesse paragraphs. Ragging is dedicated to fine-tuning paragraph edges with manual line breaks. It remedies line ends with awkward angles, curves, holes, and shapes that appear when using default settings. Rags may be active, with ample in-and-out movement from line to line, or understated, with subtle shifts. No absolute method exists. Achieve a smooth ebb and flow, and adjust anything that distracts from reading.

Before

Ragging and hyphenation are methods that finesse paragraphs. Ragging is dedicated to fine-tuning paragraph edges with manual line breaks. It remedies line ends with awkward angles, curves, holes, and shapes that appear when using default settings. Rags may be active, with ample in-and-out movement from line to line, or understated, with subtle shifts. No absolute method exists. Achieve a smooth ebb and flow, and adjust anything that distracts from reading.

After

Ragging refines paragraph edges. Awkward angles, curves, holes, and shapes that appear through default settings need tending. Rags may be active, with liberal in-and-out movement, or unassuming, with subtle variation. Hyphenation supports ragging by decisively splitting words across lines. Unwanted rivers, orphans, and widows also need special attention. Rivers are unsightly gaps or holes that appear in justified settings. Widows are one, two, or three short words on the last paragraph line. Orphans isolate single paragraph lines between pages.

Rivers and irregular spacing

Too open spacing between words, lines 1, 3, 6, and 7

Too tight spacing between words, line 5

Widow on line 8

Rivers, orphans, and widows are further factors to control when refining paragraphs. Rivers are gaps or disruptive holes that run down and across justified alignments. Widows are one, two, or three short words on the last paragraph line. They do not fill enough line length; their diminutive stature draws attention. Review and alter previous lines with effort to add heft to the last line.

Before

Rivers, orphans, and widows are further factors to control when refining paragraphs. Rivers are gaps or disruptive holes that run down and across justified alignments. Widows are one, two, or three short words on the last paragraph line. They do not fill enough line length; their diminutive stature draws attention. Review and alter previous lines with effort to add heft to the last line.

After

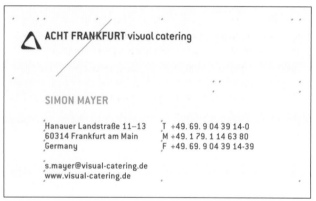

Business cards contain the Acht Frankfurt identity with the name set in sans serif Conduit. A custom typeface distinguishes the brand descriptions "digital solutions" and "visual catering." Case contrast separates the company and brand. A shared baseline with matching cap and ascender heights maintain their unity.

———

FALKO OHLMER

Hierarchy orders text by complementing and contrasting relationships. Without it, typographic design lacks focus and visual interest. Hierarchy is inherent to typesetting. Start with text when defining hierarchy. Map it by noting the quantity and variety. Rank text by importance. This defines what viewers see first, second, third, and so on. A systematic scheme unfolds that lets designers set type with purpose. The visualization of ranked text expresses hierarchy. Some elements lead; others support. Type combines cohesively and consistently to facilitate navigation. Engage viewers and direct them where to go and in what order.

Designers conduct hierarchy with typographic, spatial, and graphic factors, which offer limitless combinations to achieve variation and emphasis. Typographic factors include type size changes, style contrasts (posture, weight, and width), typeface combinations, case distinctions, and baseline shifts. For instance, a type size adjustment might be enough to differentiate basic text with few variables. Alternatively, a project might consist of three type sizes and two weights in one typeface. Headings and body text share point size and vary through a weight change or uppercase setting. Combined serif and sans serif typefaces offer more possibilities. Assign each face a function. Use their attributes to best advantage. Amplify and minimize type with appropriateness. Too few typographic factors do not distinguish; too many are redundant and complicated. Take time to build a typographic system—a well-thought-out palette of typefaces and proportional type sizes and measures, whose components interact and integrate. Systems tailored to specific text establish typesetting guidelines. When applied, repeated treatments are visual guideposts that direct viewers through projects.

Spatial and graphic factors support type for hierarchical benefit. Spatial factors include spacing (tracking, kerning, and leading), orientation shifts (horizontal, vertical, and diagonal), and position changes. For instance, leading affects the depth and typographic color of lines and paragraphs. Tight leading often projects dark impressions; open leading is optically lighter. Consider orientation shifts to juxtapose type. Rotate elements and contrast horizontal and vertical directions. Examine type positioned in close proximity versus distant. Contrast alignments, such as flush-left and -right alignments, that meet along an axis. Graphic factors including line, shape, and color also support type and aid hierarchy. Carriers or devices such as circles or squares can enclose and accentuate typographic elements. Lines direct the eye to specific type settings. Color distinguishes elements. Many options exist. Experiment and discover distinctive typesetting techniques in concert with spatial and graphic factors for best results.

The cover of a post-9/11 political study, *Transatlantic Relations in the Times of Crisis*, displays weight and color emphases to attain hierarchy. Sans serif Etica set flush left is neutral and adopts a sober personality suited to the subject matter. Strong weight contrast gives notice.

———
DAVID BŘEZINA

BASIC VARIATION AND EMPHASIS FACTORS

Typographic
Point Size
Style (Posture, Weight, Width)
Typeface Combinations
Case Distinctions
Baseline Shifts

Spatial
Spacing (Kerning, Tracking, Leading)
Orientation
Position

Graphic
Line
Shape
Color

LEVEL 1

Typeface
Thesis TheSans

Type Size
9 point

LEVEL 2

Typeface
Thesis TheSans

Type Sizes
Any combination of 8, 12, 16,
24, 48, 72, and 144 points

LEVEL 3

Typefaces
A Thesis TheSans and Century Schoolbook
B Thesis TheSans and Clarendon

Type Sizes
Any

A

B

Many methods exist to create hierarchy
and variation. Here, a series of student-
designed studies exhibits basic typographic
spatial, and graphic factors. Project objectives include hierarchical achievement,
as well as typesetting and compositional
variation. Typefaces and type sizes were
assigned for each level.

———
TYLER BROOKS

■ julian stanczak

□ ■ **august 4**, 2007–**february 11**, 2008

□ □ ■ **contemporary arts center** □ 44 east sixth street □ cincinnati, ohio □ 45202

the contemporary arts enter exhibits the work of internationally significant artist julian stanczak. polish-born stanczak trained under josef albers and conrad marca-relli at yale university's school of art and architecture. he brought this background to the art academy, where he taught from 1957–1964.

stanczak's work is characterized by *scientific precision* and the *illusion of pulsating motion*. using repeated line patterns, his work studies the optical behavior of colors in close proximity to each other. his work earned him the moniker *"father of op art."*

on lines, he writes: *"i found line—repeated line with its potent timing—paralleling many aspects of daily life. from the point of action, line behavior is distinct from color; line activates the surface of the canvas more than a single flat color. this activation of a surface through various oppositions of values and wavelengths of line in different situations, offers not a stable but an endlessly active surface, which is controlled by the range of color-fusion and tempo."*

513.345.8400 installation sponsor artist sponsors

■ **www.contemporaryartscenter.org** ■ **bartlett & co.** ■ **lpk** □ oakley & eva farris □ **mercedes-benz of cincinnati**

Weight change and orientation contrast are dominant typographic and compositional techniques. Squares support type and lead the eye to key text: title, date, location, and description. The study also features consistent lowercase settings. Slight tracking of the title "Julian Stanczak" offers subtle variation without sacrificing readability.

CONTEMPORARY ARTS CENTER
44 East Sixth Street
Cincinnati, Ohio 45202

august **4**, 2007 — *february* **11**, 2008

julian
stanczak.

The Contemporary Arts Center exhibits the work of internationally significant artist *Julian Stanczak*. Polish-born *Stanczak* trained under Josef Albers and Conrad Marca-Relli at Yale University's School of Art and Architecture. He brought this background to the Art Academy, where he taught from 1957–1964. *Stanczak*'s work is characterized by scientific precision and the illusion of pulsating motion. Using repeated line patterns, his work studies the optical behavior of colors in close proximity to each other. His work earned him the moniker *"Father of Op Art."*

On lines, he writes: **"I found line—repeated line with its potent timing—paralleling many aspects of daily life. From the point of action, line behavior is distinct from color; line activates the surface of the canvas more than a single flat color. This activation of a surface through various oppositions of values and wavelengths of line in different situations, offers not a stable but an endlessly active surface, which is controlled by the range of color-fusion and tempo."**

INSTALLATION SPONSOR

Bartlett & Co.

ARTIST SPONSORS

Mercedes-Benz of Cincinnati.
Oakley & Eva Farris.
LPK.

513 345 8400
www.contemporaryartscenter.org

Dramatic type size contrast gives attention to "Stanczak." The stem of the *k* is a leading edge for support text (location, sponsors, and contact information), which sits at flush-left and -right alignments. Bold and italic styles add typographic color in justified paragraphs. A slightly exaggerated indent signals the second paragraph.

AUGUST 4, 2007–FEBRUARY 11, 2008

Julian Stanczak

CONTEMPORARY ARTS CENTER

44 East Sixth Street
Cincinnati, Ohio 45202

www.contemporaryartscenter.org
513·345·8400

ARTIST SPONSORS
Oakley & Eva Farris
Mercedes-Benz of Cincinnati
L P K

INSTALLATION SPONSOR
Bartlett & Co.

The **Contemporary Arts Center** exhibits the work of internationally significant artist **Julian Stanczak**. Polish-born **Stanczak** trained under Josef Albers and Conrad Marca-Relli at Yale University's School of Art and Architecture. He brought this background to the Art Academy, where he taught from 1957–1964. **Stanczak's work is characterized by scientific precision and the illusion of pulsating motion. Using repeated line patterns, his work studies the optical behavior of colors in close proximity to each other. His work earned him the moniker "Father of Op Art."** *On lines, he writes: "I found line—repeated line with its potent timing—paralleling many aspects of daily life. From the point of action, line behavior is distinct from color; line activates the surface of the canvas more than a single flat color. The activation of a surface through various in different situations, offers not a stable but an endlessly active surface, which is controlled by the range of color-fusion and tempo."*

A combination of Century Schoolbook and Thesis TheSans fosters hearty typographic texture through size, posture, weight, and case shifts. The typefaces mix effectively in the paragraph. Such variation rich with typographic color calls attention to sentences.

KUOW

PUGET SOUND PUBLIC RADIO
2008 REPORT TO CONTRIBUTORS

CAR TALK

WEEKEND EDITION

THE DIANE REHM SHOW

BBC WORLD SERVICE

MARKETPLACE

A PRAIRIE HOME COMPANION

KUOW NEWS

KUOW PRESENTS

WEEKDAY

THE CONVERSATION

SPEAKER'S FORUM

SOUND FOCUS

THE SWING YEARS AND BEYOND

MORNING EDITION

TO THE POINT

DAY TO DAY

ALL THINGS CONSIDERED

AS IT HAPPENS

WAIT, WAIT...DON'T TELL ME!

THIS AMERICAN LIFE

THE WORLD

The annual report cover for KUOW, the NPR affiliate radio station in Seattle, features the typeface Bau. A durable uppercase setting with vertical orientation echoes the image on which it rises up like a radio tower.

———

CHENG DESIGN

A baseline shift is a change in type position above or below the baseline. "Reisz" in the Allison Reisz Photography logotype set in the typeface Chalet (Paris 1970 and 1980) shifts above the baseline. The change is subtle and offers distinction.

———

LUXECETERA

Multiple typefaces shape the Bun Mee logotype, which features a customized version of Refrigerator Deluxe with Banque Gothique. A third typeface, Numbers Depot, appears in "2010." Relationships among typefaces contrast with personality. Vintage, hand-painted letterforms inspired the typeface selections.

———

MINE™

The cover of *Beer: A Genuine Collection of Cans* contains three levels of hierarchy: title, subtitle, and author names. Contrasting point sizes in the serif typeface Freight creates hierarchy. An interior spread shows a similar three-level structure with a heading, body text, and caption. Simple size shifts with position changes achieve order.

—

DAN BECKER
LANCE WILSON

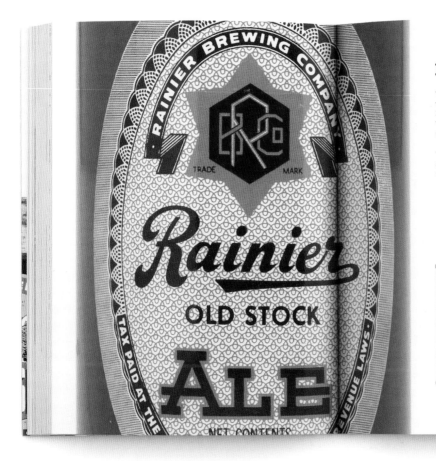

Rainier

The history of Rainier beer dates back to 1878 when it was first brewed in Seattle, Washington. In 1916, alcoholic beverages were outlawed in Washington State, and as a result, Rainier moved to San Francisco until Prohibition ended.

Throughout its history, Rainier was produced by several different breweries. The brand survives to this day under the ownership of Pabst.

Rainier Brewing Co.
San Francisco, CA | 1940s

269

Adept typesetting involves studied principles and practice plus keen observation and treatment. Aesthetic tailoring is the final typesetting phase when designing with type for communication. Called microtypography, it ensures refined type settings. Projects are free of distractions and missteps that inhibit reading and message delivery. All mediums and formats require an enhanced sensitivity to typographic detail. Presented here are fundamental etiquette factors that offer simple methods to tailor type.

Maintain proper typeface proportions. Use only available styles—posture, weight, and width— of chosen typefaces, which have been carefully considered and proportioned by type designers. Select italic or oblique fonts from within the typeface. Avoid altering roman styles by slanting, thus creating objectionable "fake italics." Adding strokes to vary type weight is poor practice. It is inadvisable to skew or stretch letterforms to make narrow or wide alternatives. Proper proportions and typeface integrity are diminished.

Maintain baseline relationships. Baselines are imaginary lines on which letterforms, words, lines, and paragraphs sit. Letterforms maintain shared baselines, which support left to right reading patterns. Stacking type breaks the natural reading flow. Shift orientation, if vertical presence is desired. Type reads up or down with intact baseline relationships.

Match combined typefaces optically when set side by side. When setting multiple typefaces, carefully review the size relationships between them. Match them optically, not by point size. At the same size, one typeface can look larger or smaller than another set side by side.

Choose roman (or regular) brackets, curly brackets, and parentheses. Brackets, curly brackets, and parentheses remain upright (roman or regular) even if the text inside them is italic.

italic   *fake italic*   fake italic

weight   **fake weight**

width   fake width   **fake width**

m m   combined typefaces

54-point Epic and Alright Sans   18-point Epic and 16.5-point Alright Sans

{*italic*}   [*italic*]   (*italic*)

fi fi fl fl

SMALL CAPS   FULL CAPS

SMALL CAPS   FAKE SMALL CAPS

SMALL CAPS   lowercase

A A a B B b

forty-five	break-ing	1900–2000	31–36
NOT	NOT	NOT	NOT
forty—five	break-ing	1900-2000	31—36

"When I'm working on a problem,
I never think about beauty. I think
only how to solve the problem.
But when I have finished, if the
solution is not beautiful, I know
it is wrong."

· R. Buckminster Fuller

Before

"When I'm working on a problem,
I never think about beauty. I think
only how to solve the problem.
But when I have finished, if the
solution is not beautiful, I know
it is wrong."

· R. Buckminster Fuller

After

Insert ligatures and avoid character collisions.
A ligature is the union of two or more characters
into one. Varieties include stylistic, lexical, and
discretionary. Become familiar with typefaces
and know ligature availability. If they exist, use
them. If they do not, be attentive to character
collisions and kern aptly.

Use small caps only if offered in typefaces selected.
Small caps are uniquely designed letterforms that
share a similar weight and x-height with lowercase
(SMALL CAPS are typically slightly taller). When
elements such as acronyms and abbreviations
appear in body text, SMALL CAPS replace FULL
CAPITALS, which are optically too large next
to lowercase . Use SMALL CAPS only if offered
in a selected typeface—not all contain them.
Simply reducing full caps to small-cap size makes
them look too thin and narrow. "Fake small caps"
are awkward and discordant. SMALL CAPS also
require open tracking.

Use hyphens and dashes appropriately. Hyphens (-)
appear in breaking (break-ing) and compound words
(forty-five, well-equipped). En dashes (–) link items
such as dates (1900–2000), times (8:00–9:00), and
page numbers (31–36). Extra space is unneeded before
and after en dashes. Kern to avoid accidental collisions.
Em dashes (—) separate thoughts. No spaces are
needed before and after—though kerning can pertain.
En dashes can replace em dashes when separating
thoughts. In such cases, space before and after the
en dash is required. Regardless of the method, use
them aptly and consistently.

Refine punctuation. Slight, distracting spaces form
when punctuation marks such as periods, commas,
and quotation marks sit along flush edges. Manual
modifications that position such marks outside flush
edges ensure optical alignment. Hanging punctuation applies to (noting a few) asterisks, apostrophes,
commas, periods, and quotation marks. Other marks
that share visual weight with characters such as
question marks and exclamation points typically
do not need attention.

Use correct apostrophes, quotation marks, and primes.
True apostrophes (single quotes) and quotation marks
(double quotes) are curved or angled, open or closed.
They are not straight up-and-down forms, which commonly appear by default in place of correct marks.
Keyboards provide one key for two sets of symbols—
left (open) and right (closed) apostrophes and quotation marks. Typing the assigned key makes ambidex-
trous, typewriter-style, straight, or dumb single and
double marks. Recognize the difference between true
and fake forms. Ensure accurate use and manually
substitute proper forms through glyph menus. The
option to turn on "smart quotes" exists in software
applications, which eases the process altogether
through automatic replacement. Prime marks, which
are typically straight or angled, represent measures
such as feet and inches, minutes and seconds, and
arcseconds and arcminutes.

- Balance bullets optically or substitute midpoints.
  No adjustments.

- Bullets are common typographic devices that identify list items.
  Reduced 1.25 points with a slight baseline shift up (0.5 pt).

· Midpoints are smaller bullet alternatives.
  No adjustments.

Balance bullets optically or substitute midpoints.
Bullets are common typographic devices that
identify list items. Hung outside alignments,
bullets often appear too large next to type set
at the same size. Thus, slight point size reduction
serves them well. Baseline shifts (type position
changes above or below the baseline) optically
balance bullet position adjacent to text.
Midpoints are smaller bullet alternatives that
require no size adjustments for optical fit.

Word space?··Insert one space between sentences.

Word space?·Insert one space between sentences.

Insert one word space between sentences. Only one
word space between sentences is required. Double
spaces add extra, unwanted white space between
sentences that distract. Punctuation followed by
a single word space plus the next sentence start
(typically with a capital) offer enough visual cues
that render useless the double space.

Refine paragraph and line edges. Ragging refines
paragraph and line edges. Awkward angles, curves, holes,
and shapes that appear through default settings
require tending. Rags may be active, with
liberal in-and-out movement, or unassuming, with
subtle variation.

Refine paragraph and line edges. Ragging refines
paragraph and line edges. Awkward angles, curves,
holes, and shapes that appear through default
settings require tending. Rags may be active, with
liberal in-and-out movement, or unassuming,
with subtle variation.

Before

After

Unwanted rivers, orphans, and widows also require special attention. Rivers are unsightly gaps or holes that appear in justified settings. Widows are one, two, or three short words on the last paragraph line.

Proper Words	syllables		
Proper Words	syl-lables	into	hyphen-ation
NOT	NOT	NOT	NOT
Prop-er Words	syll-ables	in-to	hy-phenation

Kerning

Typography

Before

Typography

After

UPPERCASE

condensed

Before

UPPERCASE

condensed

After

Avoid tracking lowercase and paragraphs (continuous text). Lowercase settings typically need minimal to no tracking because of their shape variation. Words, lines, and paragraphs loosely, tightly, or negatively tracked no longer read as intended.

Before

Fix rivers, orphans, and widows. Unwanted rivers, orphans, and widows also require special attention. Rivers are unsightly gaps or holes that appear in justified settings. Widows are one, two, or three short words on the last paragraph line. Orphans isolate single paragraph lines between pages.

Control hyphenation. Hyphenation splits words across lines to improve typographic appearance. Watch consecutive hyphenations at line ends— there should be no more than two in a row. Avoid hyphenating proper names and nouns. The first and last full paragraph lines are hyphen free. Break words into correct syllables. Avoid hyphenating words with less than five letterforms. Split words down the middle in best cases. Too little left behind or brought ahead is awkward. A rule of thumb is two letterforms behind, three ahead.

Kern between characters. Attentive type setting monitors unwanted collisions or gaps that distract. Kerning adjusts the slivers of space between characters. Such fixes are common with letterforms next to T, V, W, and Y. Delicate shifts closer to or farther from one another remedy awkward combinations. Numerals, especially those paired with 1, require care, as do punctuation marks including dashes, parentheses, and backslashes. Character space increases at large type sizes and makes errors more apparent.

Track specific settings. Tracking alters the overall spacing of words, lines, and paragraphs to enhance readability. Uppercase settings (full and small caps) and lining numeral sequences rely on open tracking for recognition. Condensed typefaces with narrow proportions and counters in upper and lowercase can benefit from slight tracking.

Avoid tracking lowercase and paragraphs (continuous text). Lowercase settings typically need minimal to no tracking because of their shape variation. Words, lines, and paragraphs loosely, tightly, or negatively tracked no longer read as intended.

After

5

STRUCTURE

Structure shapes typographic compositions and offers designers creative potential. Used to order, connect, and balance, structure helps designers build rational layouts. Harmony follows with clarity and aesthetic grace. Viewers engage in and navigate works without distraction. Structural systems are mathematic, mechanical, intuitive, and organic. Designers construct them differently based on function, experience, and preference. Inspiration exists in architecture, art, geometry, music, and nature. All areas offer methods worthy of in-depth discovery. For instance, research classic proportion systems such as the golden section, divine proportion, and root rectangle. Study the findings of mathematicians, artists, and designers such as Fibonacci, Leonardo da Vinci, and Le Corbusier. Explore grid systems comprised of vertical and horizontal spatial divisions. Rely on intuition and allow connections between typographic elements to assist decision-making. Regardless of the plan on which the structure derives, the goal is communication through typographic design. Use structure to achieve it.

Boundless options exist to divide compositional space and distribute content. Shared here are basic structures with a focus on grids and alternate methods suitable for typographic design. The objective is to provide examples that foster success on macrotypographic levels.[1] Fundamental structures are adaptable and responsive skeletal supports critical to composition. They guide the layout process yet remain unnoticed in final works; their form need not be apparent to viewers. Content and context drive structural development. As in choosing typefaces and typesetting, first analyze text and understand it. Identify the users and viewing conditions. Define the medium and its parameters. Make structures that satisfy conditions and best support the content. Solid frameworks generate inviting physical or virtual canvases ready to explore. Synthesize in them typographic elements and white space. Control positions and refine alignments, and creative and clear communication will follow. Aptly built and exercised structures give viewers the subconscious sense that compositions feel right.

SELECTED READINGS

Design Elements: Form & Space
Dennis M. Puhalla, Ph.D.

Geometry of Design:
Studies in Proportion and Composition
Kimberly Elam

The Power of Limits:
Proportional Harmonies in Nature,
Art, and Architecture
Gyorgy Doczi

1 Macrotypography addresses composition or layout— the plan and organization of typographic elements. Key considerations include spatial positioning and relationship building among elements and white space. Microtypography refers to typesetting essentials and details. Principal micro factors include spacing and aesthetic tailoring (see chapter 1).

Baselines are imaginary lines on which letterforms, words, lines, and paragraphs sit. Baseline alignment refers to a calculated system of horizontal guides at equally spaced vertical intervals that underlie typographic layouts. A baseline alignment system designates related positions for all type regardless of the range of point sizes. Baselines enable consistent horizontal alignment across compositions. Lines of type coincide; they also back up from page to page if viewed one atop another. Vertical rhythm and typographic unity are compositional goals. Baseline alignment helps achieve them. Body text leading (the vertical distance from one baseline to the next measured in points) typically regulates baseline intervals. For instance, if body text leading is 10 point, set a 10-point baseline alignment system. Leading for other elements follows in multiples of 10 (20, 30, 40, and so on). If a stricter interval is desired, an alternative is a 5-point baseline grid with multiples of 5 (10, 15, 20, and so on). Take the time to build baseline alignment systems. They aid typographic decision-making and structural development. Baseline intervals also influence margin size or grid module height. They can inform positions of elements such as illustrations or photographs that accompany type. Baseline alignment systems are reliable control factors suited for all projects. Order is evident to viewers, even if sensed intuitively.

The Grid System website features multiple columns and baseline alignment. Text set in Helvetica shares a common baseline interval that marks typographic position. A considered vertical grid structure with a horizontal baseline alignment system fosters order, connection, and balance.

ANTONIO CARUSONE

STRUCTURE *Baseline Alignment*

CONTENTS

CONTENTS

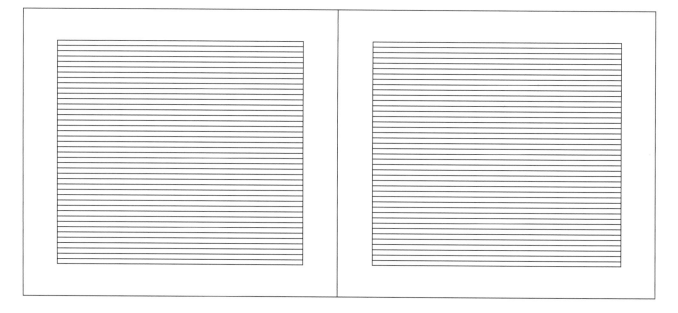

A 12-point baseline alignment system underlies the *International Drawing Annual*. Body text in the serif face Mercury is set at 9/12 (9-point type over 12-point leading). Sans serif typefaces Gotham and Knockout in various point sizes have leading in multiples of 12 (24, 36, 48, and so on). Margins also fit the system at 72-point.

———

AUGUST BUREAU

23

TRAVIS
TOWNSEND

Lexington, Kentucky

THE ACTIVITY OF DRAWING | The activity of drawing first enters the creation of my work in the form of small doodles. I consistently, and perhaps obsessively, sketch abstract shapes, dead little birdies, and designs for contraptions. I formulate these into ideas for objects, often on odd scraps of household paper. Sometimes these doodles evolve into finished works, and other times they merely serve to document an idea. Sketches pervasively accumulate in my office, at home, and in the studio, and inform, but don't necessarily dictate, my making. Many also find their way into the interior spaces and onto the surfaces of my objects.

Clamping pieces of wood together impermanently, I am able to look at the overall composition and then decide on changes. I might shorten boards or stack together a variety of linear parts to three-dimensionally draw out objects. This process of sculpting is similar to sketching, and like a worked-over, much erased sketch, the completed sculptures have linear elements that vary in intensity, gesture, and movement. I consider each piece of material to be a small component to the whole, like marks making up a drawing.

RENOVATED FLIGHTLESS DEVICES | My idiosyncratic sculptures play off the forms and function of tools, toys, boats, and, perhaps, military equipment. These process-oriented works take a winding path to completion, evolving from continuously redrawn sketches and traveling through many transformations before being cut apart, reassembled, and reworked. Parts are often transplanted, left behind, or recycled. Through this method of construction and reconstruction, I am able to intuitively build and then, at a later time, make necessary changes.

Embracing the unplanned, these oddly familiar, nearly useful-looking sculptures are imbued with human characteristics and gestures. Curious inspection and patient observation reveal previously unseen drawings and room-like interiors, many with small chairs and ladders 'left over' from previous inhabitants. These things have handles, openings, drawn symbols, and moveable parts, but like the mystery of a ritual object from a broken-down culture, the physical or metaphorical functions are left to the imagination. In an increasingly commercialized, displaced society, I'm attempting to build slow, somewhat clumsy, objects that reveal a layered history.

Raft for .... (with Constellation Drawing) is the most recent permutation of a work that has been slowly transforming for eleven years and continues my experimentation with connecting the sculptures to wall drawings. My hope is that viewers will fill in the blank and finish the narrative for themselves. Who inhabited this craft and from what were they fleeing? Another *TANKARD (4th Permutation, with Boarded-up Cloud Drawing)* and *Tankship (with Infection Drawing)* are two other works that, among other associations, suggest a narrative about the society that once operated (and controlled the drawings of) these deserted vessels/devices. ◆

THE GAP IN DRAWING

HELEN BARFF
London, United Kingdom
Artist
Camberwell College of Art, M.A. in Drawing, 2004
Goldsmiths College, B.A. in Fine Art and Art History (honors), 1999

TO DRAW IS TO LOOK,
BUT HERE I PROPOSE THAT WITHIN THAT OBSERVATION
IS A MOMENT OF BLINDNESS
THAT IS CRUCIAL TO THE MOTIVATION TO DRAW.

references
Derrida, Jacques. *Memoirs of the Blind: The Self-Portrait and Other Ruins.*
Translated by Pascale-Anne Brault and Michael Naas.
Chicago: The University of Chicago Press, 1993.
bibliography
Derrida, Jacques. *Memoirs of the Blind: The Self-Portrait and Other Ruins.*
Translated by Pascale-Anne Brault and Michael Naas.
Chicago: The University of Chicago Press, 1993.
Lyotard, Jean-François. *Postmodern Fables.*
Translated by Georges Van Den Abbeele.
Minneapolis: University of Minnesota Press, 1997.
Townsend, Chris. *New Art from London.* London: Thames and Hudson, 2006.
Camberwell College of Arts / University of the Arts /
St Marys NHS Trust / Imperial College, 2004.
How Do You Look? [online]. Available from: http://www.howdoyoulook.co.uk/
[Cited February 2007].

Pliny the Elder states the origin of drawing as when Butades traces the shadow of her departing lover on the wall, but she isn't looking at him, she is looking at his shadow. There is always a gap in drawing; you can't look at the subject and the mark on the page at the same time. As Derrida writes in *Memoirs of the Blind*: 'Butades does not see her lover, ...it is as if seeing were forbidden in order to draw, as if one drew only on the condition of not seeing. Whether Butades follows the traits of a shadow or a silhouette— her hand sometimes guided by Cupid,— or whether she draws on the surface of a wall or on a veil, a skiagraphia or shadow writing in each case inaugurates an art of blindness. From the outset, perception belongs to recollection. ...Detached from the present of perception, fallen from the thing itself—which is thus divided—a shadow is a simultaneous memory, and Butades' stick is a staff of the blind.' (pp. 49–51)

Saccades are the fast movement of the eyes between fixed points. We don't see a whole scene at once. The eye moves between these various points within the scene. Saccadic masking, or suppression, is a procedure where the mind blocks visual processing during eye movements. Neither the motion of the eye, or any blur in the image, nor the gap in visual perception is noticeable to the viewer. Between looking and drawing we encounter this visual masking. In this gap we don't see, we remember.

At the centre of our vision, where the nerves hit the retina is a blind spot, we don't see anything; the brain fills in the information. Our brains contain a visual index that is built from memory, used to fill the gaps in vision.

Vision therefore carries in it something unseen, something mute. A drawing contains a trace of a subject. A subject is located in front of the drawer but in the act of making the drawn mark it is unseen. Between the subject and its representative mark on the page is a distance or 'blind gap' that relies on a memory of the subject.

Drawing is a blind gesture from within vision. It exists in the space between looking, where things are remembered and forgotten. This gesture contains a lament. In the touch of drawing on a surface, whether harsh or gentle, there is a reassurance in this contact. Drawing is instant, direct. It answers back as promptly and unaccompanied as the sound of a voice. It gives an enduring answer to being temporary.

Is there gaps in vision that provokes the reason to draw. Although all about looking, drawing happens in moments between looking. We draw to try and see through the blindness. We draw to try and remember the gaps. ◆

"THE GRID

does not automatically ensure an exciting solution. The designer must still

exercise all the experience at his command: discretion, timing, and a sense

of drama and sequence. In brief, the intelligent designer will recognize

that the grid can help him achieve harmony and order, but also that it may

be abandoned when and if necessary. To function successfully, the grid

system, like all workable systems, must be interpreted as freely as necessary.

It is this very freedom which adds richness and a note of surprise to what

might otherwise be potentially lifeless."

from A Designer's Art

PAUL RAND

SELECTED READINGS

Grid Systems in Graphic Design
Josef Müller-Brockmann

Making and Breaking the Grid
Tim Samara

Grid systems are vertical and horizontal divisions of space that structure compositions. They offer multiple position and sizing options for typographic elements. Grids promote clarity and consistency and make designing with type efficient. They help designers organize information and users navigate layouts. Proportional relationships between typographic elements emerge naturally. Invisible sightlines create connections up, down, and across layouts. Alignment fosters harmony. In *A Designer's Art*, Paul Rand wisely explains grid use: "The grid does not automatically ensure an exciting solution. The designer must still exercise all the experience at his command: discretion, timing, and a sense of drama and sequence. In brief, the intelligent designer will recognize that the grid can help him achieve harmony and order, but also that it may be abandoned when and if necessary. To function successfully, the grid system, like all workable systems, must be interpreted as freely as necessary. It is this very freedom which adds richness and a note of surprise to what might otherwise be potentially lifeless."

Designers customize grids based on content assessment and typographic settings; their breadth and quantity define them. Flexible, not restrictive, grids accommodate diverse typographic elements across mediums. Adaptable factors, not absolutes, lead their development and application. Use grids to express text best. Break them in service to it. Proficiency develops with practice.

A simple three-column grid fosters consistency in Neenah Paper's Against the Grain website. Such grids are well suited to works with changing content, which can rest in one column or span many. Sans serif Avenir distinguishes headings, subheads are Helvetica; body text is in Times.

———

RULE29

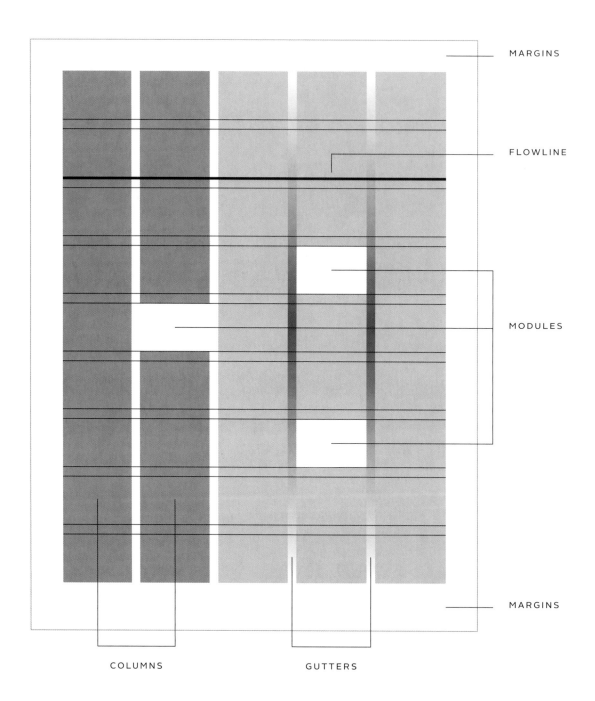

MARGINS

FLOWLINE

MODULES

MARGINS

COLUMNS

GUTTERS

Grids guide typographic layouts. Vertical and horizontal spatial divisions offer multiple alignment and sizing choices. Used effectively by designers, grids nurture order, connection, and balance. Grids are developed after a careful analysis of content and context. They accommodate all compositional components comfortably.

Columns
Columns are vertical guides that split space into segments. Framed by margins, columns divide the active area and offer positioning options. Single-column grids are best suited for works with continuous text. Multiple-column grids serve projects with many typographic variables and elements, such as illustrations or photographs.

Gutters
Gutters are thin channels of white space that separate columns and rows. Their size typically equals body-text leading or the baseline alignment interval. Gutters prevent collisions when elements juxtapose.

Flowlines
Flowlines (hang lines) are limited horizontal guides that indicate where key elements rise or hang. For instance, one flowline might set the consistent starting position of body text; another might define the heading location.

Margins
Margins define the active compositional area where typographic elements dwell. They are a buffer between live content and format edges. Margins also deliver essential white space (or breathing room) that frames layouts and directs the eye to positive areas.

Modules
Modules are active spaces occupied by elements and white space, which fill single modules or cross many. Modules are square or rectangular, with horizontal or vertical stress (wide versus tall). A set of modules forms a spatial zone.

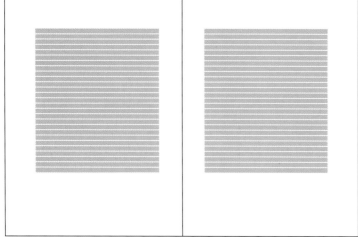

Single-column grids are structural systems suited for continuous text. Framing the body text is the central factor. Balance relationships between type size, line length, and leading for extended reading. Symmetry offers balance, asymmetry variation.

Single-column grids are simple structures suited for works with continuous text (running paragraphs). Examples include journals and novels. Such frameworks also serve text-rich websites, such as blogs. Single-column grids are devoted to framing a text block. Margins—left and right, top and bottom, inner and outer (for spreads)—define the active area and provide white space. Margin size varies per text and project dimensions. Wide margins typically maintain reader focus. Generous space creates an open environment minus peripheral distraction. Books and some multiple-page publications benefit from full margins that provide ample finger room to hold them. Small margins extend active layout space and host more content. They can also produce apt compositional tension because of the proximity of elements to format edges. (Small margins are typically useful for multiple column and modular grids with varied text and image.) Inner margins in publications where pages meet at a center spine demand deliberation to avoid lost content.

To make single-column grids, first resolve the ideal paragraph setting, which balances type size, line length, and leading (see chapter 4). Readability and comfort level are essential. Multiples of the body-text leading (or baseline alignment interval) can shape margin size. Spatial divisions then share proportions. If included in the text, variables, such as footers and footnotes, affect margins because they typically reside in them. Margin space must accommodate such elements with the text block. Identify typographic variables and their settings before making decisions. Nurture optimal conditions for extended reading and handling in all mediums. Be flexible. Modify measures as necessary through the layout process.

STILLSTAND
DER ERZÄHLTEN ZEIT
René Zechlin

Das Theaterstück *Les Noces d'Arlequin* von Carlo Bertinazzi stand von 1761 bis 1779 ununterbrochen auf dem Spielplan der Pariser Comédie Italienne. Zur Beliebtheit des Stücks trug sicherlich die Integration des Gemäldes *L'Accordée de Village* (*Die Dorfbraut*, 1761) von Jean-Baptiste Greuze bei, das zu den bekanntesten Bildern der damaligen Zeit und zu den Hauptattraktionen des Louvre gehörte. In der Mitte des zweiten Aktes hob sich der Vorhang, und das Publikum erkannte das Gemälde in Form eines schauspielerischen Standbildes wieder. Diese erste überlieferte Aufführung eines Tableau vivant, der Nachstellung eines Gemäldes mit unbeweglich verharrenden Darstellern, war gleichzeitig eine Überlagerung unterschiedlicher Darstellungs- und Erzählformen in Malerei, Literatur und Theater. So wurde das lebende Standbild durch einen Harlekin gestört, der die Darstellung des Gemäldes durchschritt und sie kommentierte. Die Idee des Tableau vivant, das vom späten 18. bis zur Mitte des 19. Jahrhunderts als gesellschaftliche Unterhaltung in privaten Salons äußerst beliebt war, basierte „auf der Vorstellung, beim Gemälde handele es sich gewissermaßen um ein ‚angehaltenes' Zeitbild, das nur in Körperlichkeit rückübersetzt werden bräuchte, um wieder ganz und gar lebendig zu sein." Denis Diderot griff die Darstellungsform von Bertinazzi in seiner Theatertheorie von 1758 auf. „Die Rolle, die er dem Lebenden Bild dabei zuerkennt, ist die

[1] Joanna Barck, *Hin zum Film – Zurück zu den Bildern: Tableaux Vivants: „Lebende Bilder" in Filmen von Antamoro, Korda, Visconti und Pasolini*, Bielefeld, 2008, S. 13.

14

STANDSTILL
OF NARRATED TIME
René Zechlin

Carlo Bertinazzi's play *Les Noces d'Arlequin* had an uninterrupted run from 1761 until 1779 at Paris' Comédie Italienne. Surely one reason for the play's popularity was the inclusion of the painting *L'Accordée de Village* (*The Village Bride*, 1761) by Jean-Baptiste Greuze, which was among the most famous paintings of the period and one of the main attractions at the Louvre. In the middle of the second act, the curtain rose, and the audience saw the painting reenacted in the form of a theatrical scene. This first known performance of a tableau vivant, the reenactment of a painting with actors frozen in place, was at the same time an overlapping of various forms of representation and narrative in painting, literature, and theater. This tableau vivant was thus disturbed by a harlequin who walks through the scene commenting upon it. The idea of the tableau vivant, which was extremely popular as a form of entertainment in private salons from the late eighteenth to the mid-nineteenth centuries, was based "on the notion that a painting was in a certain sense a 'frozen' picture in time that only needed to be translated back to physicality to become entirely animate." Denis Diderot took up Bertinazzi's mode of representation in his theory of the theater: "The role granted to the tableau vivant is that of a positively understood interruption or break in the plot [...] Interrupting the acting by freezing the scene, the attention of the spectator is to be drawn to particular matter, and the scene was removed from

[1] Joanna Barck, *Hin zum Film – Zurück zu den Bildern: Tableaux Vivants: „Lebende Bilder" in Filmen von Antamoro, Korda, Visconti und Pasolini*, (Bielefeld, 2008), 13.

15

A catalog spread for artist Omer Fast employs a single-column grid. Plentiful margins define the active text area and provide room to hold the piece. Justified body text contains German and English essays differentiated by sans serif Metallophile and serif De Walpergen Pica (Fell Types).

PROJECT PROJECTS

Multiple-column grids range from two-column structures to intricate varieties with eight, twelve, sixteen, and more spatial divisions. They are fit for projects across mediums with diverse text and factors, such as images, charts, and tables. Creating multiple-column grids follows simple steps that adapt per project and designer preference. The first step is choosing layout dimensions that best support the content. They are neither too small, making for tight quarters; nor too big, engulfing elements in space. Using standard sizes is a good starting point. They are established dimensions that accommodate content with economic efficiency. For example, a now common website width of 960 pixels is divisible by 2, 3, 4, 5, 6, 8, 10, 12, and so on. This flexibility offers many grid options. Confirm current dimensions for mobile devices or tablets, because digital formats advance quickly. The North American and International Standard Organization (ISO) provides standard paper sizes for print works.

With the dimensions set, define the margins. They frame the usable composition space and provide buffers between content and format edges. They also offer essential white space (or breathing room) that activates layouts and directs the eye to content. The allocation and proportion of white space is equal in compositional value to type. It is a considered factor in the layout process. Margin size varies with every project. Ample margins provide open canvases that surround content liberally. Small margins offer more usable space, which is ideal for complex projects. Close connections between elements and format edges add tension that benefits some works. Review existing designs for inspiration. Acquire a sense of what works in varied formats and mediums.

Columns are regions dedicated to positioning type and other elements. They are created by dividing the area inside the margins into equally distributed vertical regions. Quantity and width varies to suit content and type settings. Too many columns can stifle decisiveness; limited numbers restrict invention. More columns typically offer flexibility through multiple alignment points. Using a primary element as a guide is one tactic to divide space. It ensures the grid accommodates it. For example, two to three columns can provide ample width to contain the body text, with the captions fitting one column. Make spatial divisions that hold everything.

Next, add intervals, called gutters, between the columns. Gutters are thin channels of white space that separate columns and prevent collisions. If text and image sit side by side, a gutter is the spatial pause where text ends and image begins. Gutters also separate paragraphs if set directly next to one another. A typical gutter measure equals the body-text leading or the baseline alignment interval. As a final grid-building step, consider adding horizontal flowlines (hang lines). Unlike baselines that underlie layouts top to bottom, flowlines are limited guides that reference where key elements rise or hang. One flowline might define the consistent starting position of body text; another might mark heading location. Use baselines to inform flowline location.

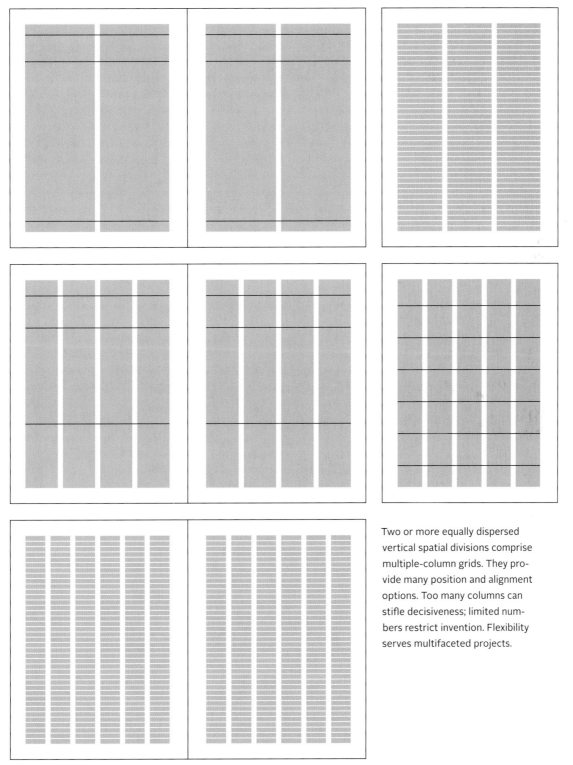

Two or more equally dispersed vertical spatial divisions comprise multiple-column grids. They provide many position and alignment options. Too many columns can stifle decisiveness; limited numbers restrict invention. Flexibility serves multifaceted projects.

The ᴇᴄᴏ book cover is spacious and inviting. It sets the tone for the interior spreads. Sans serif face ᴅɪɴ has large counters and thin uniform strokes. The title is large in scale, yet its openness does not conceal the photograph; it suggests a window looking out to sea.

An eight-column grid is the basis of the interior spreads. Multiple columns are flexible and support all text in ᴅɪɴ and Memphis, as well as photographs. Consistency arises because spatial divisions have common proportions.

———

BLØK DESIGN

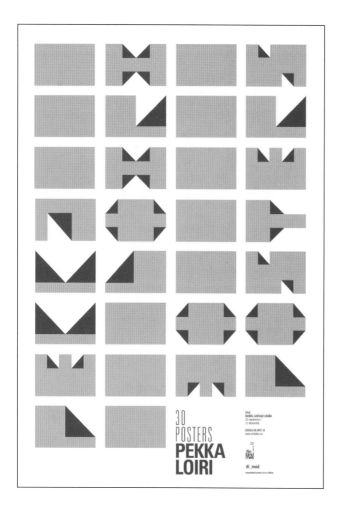

Modular grids are suitable for multifaceted projects in any medium. They have equally distributed spatial modules vertically and horizontally—a precise system of columns and rows. Modules are active spaces in which type and elements such as illustrations and photographs reside. Content can fill single modules or cross many in any direction. Combined modules form spatial zones. Depending on composition size, modules can be square or rectangular, with horizontal or vertical stress (wide versus tall). Average paragraph line length and leading, as well as key image dimensions, can regulate module proportion and stress. Be certain the modules contain the dominant elements to their best advantage. Baseline alignment intervals can also define module height. Multiple modules offer flexibility and alignment options. Too few modules limit positioning and scaling choices; too many cloud decision-making. Test the options. Find the right balance in accord with content. Modular grids, like multiple-column grids, also have intervals between modules called gutters. Gutters are buffers for juxtaposed type and other elements. Body text leading or baselines typically inform gutter size. Modular grids are easy-to-build structures that adapt across mediums through consistent module proportion, regardless of layout dimensions. This flexibility makes modular grids useful for projects with components in different media.

Color-filled rectangles make a modular grid instantly evident. Although grids are typically unseen, the structure defines the design and adds graphic interest. Custom letterforms fit into modules and spell "Pekka Loiri 30 Posters." Two modules contain informative text in Univers Condensed.

———

LSDSPACE

Building modular grids starts with dividing the compositional space in half vertically. Proceed horizontally. Subdivide space equally until a desired module proportion and quantity forms that best supports content. Add intervals called gutters between modules to separate them.

Alternate methods offer compositional options beyond traditional grids. The lack of preset spatial divisions nurtures intuition and experimentation. Inspired by improvisation, axiality, and geometry, alternate methods best suit projects with limited text—letterforms, words, and lines; paragraphs or multiple-page sequential formats can pose challenges. Improvised methods use type as alignment edges and points, which form as the designer positions it in the space. Connections between elements govern decision-making. For instance, if one letterform, word, or line shifts position, others follow. Designers compose type organically. It is a responsive process. Like grids, alignment fosters harmony. Elements depend on one another to decide location and attain compositional balance. Such spontaneity aids designers who find it rigid to begin working with a grid. In the inspiring words of Josef Albers: "To experiment is at first more valuable than to produce; free play in the beginning develops courage."[2]

A right-facing folio from the GreenLight Fund 5 Year Progress Report shows an improvised structure formed by typographic bonds in Akzidenz-Grotesk. Letterforms, words, and lines create alignment points and guides that define units and structure the page.

———

MONDERER DESIGN

2 Bayer, Herbert, Walter Gropius, and Ise Gropius, eds. *Bauhaus 1919–1928*. New York: The Museum of Modern Art, 1938.

Improvised methods inform the design of some logotypes. Connections between letter-forms and words advise alignment; they rely on their structure to achieve balance. Logotypes are compact, independent units with aesthetic vigor that stand strongly. A medley of type-faces echoes celebration and diversity in a logotype that marks the centennial at the Faculty of Humanities, University of Lisbon, Portugal. The logotype functions at small and large sizes. Its rectilinear alignments fit its use on the building façade.

—

FBA.

Two perpendicular axes structure
the *Typeface* film poster. A vertical
axis stems from the *I* of OBRAZI
ČRK (typeface in Slovene). It defines
the flush edge for type. Weight and
posture variations in Univers aid
typographic hierarchy.

——
TOMATO KOŠIR

Using a single axis, or a relationship between two axes, offers composition methods pertinent to works with limited text. A simple typographic structure develops by placing one line—an axis—in a composition. The axis is a guide. It provides immediate alignment edges and points for type. For example, start with one vertical axis. Divide a composition in half with it. A basic structure with a centered, symmetrical axis appears. Type may extend from the left and right sides of the axis. Move the axis up, down, left, or right. An asymmetrical structure emerges; type attains a decisive horizontal or vertical emphasis. Rotate the axis ninety degrees. Elements shift in orientation. They can be turned vertically or can hang from or rise above the axis. Spin the axis another thirty or forty-five degrees for a dynamic diagonal scheme. Type might sit along the diagonal axis or stem from either side of it. Adding a second axis adds complexity. Make it parallel or perpendicular to the first axis. The point where two axes meet is a focal point. Proximity to a focal point aids hierarchy. Simple structures suitable for limited text need not be complicated.

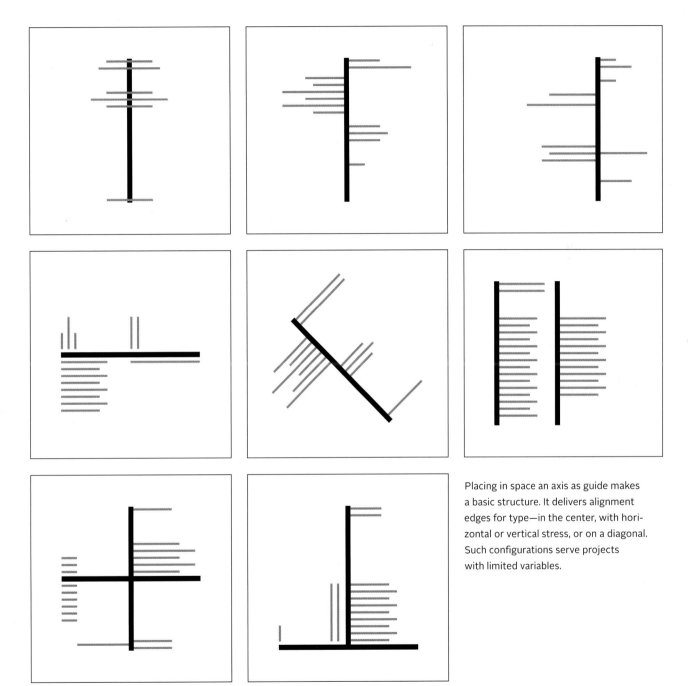

Placing in space an axis as guide makes a basic structure. It delivers alignment edges for type—in the center, with horizontal or vertical stress, or on a diagonal. Such configurations serve projects with limited variables.

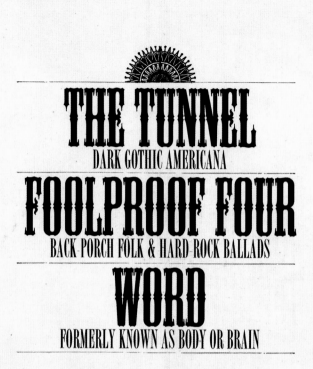

THE TUNNEL
DARK GOTHIC AMERICANA

FOOLPROOF FOUR
BACK-PORCH FOLK & HARD-ROCK BALLADS

WORD
FORMERLY KNOWN AS BODY OR BRAIN

APPEARING LIVE! AT THE BOTTOM OF THE HILL 1233 17TH STREET
WEDNESDAY FEBRUARY SECOND, 2011
9:00 PM, 8.00 DOLLARS

A central axis structures the print
for The Tunnel, Foolproof Four,
and Word. Ornamental typefaces
Mesquite and Bordeaux create
ambiance. A symmetrical layout with
limited text that expresses proper
mood and apt typesetting does
not need structural complexity
to be successful.

———

PATRICK L CRAWFORD DESIGN

Typographic elements stem from the left and right sides of a slightly off-center, single axis. Spatial dimension adds depth and character. A custom designed typeface amplifies style.

———

MIRKO ILIĆ CORP.

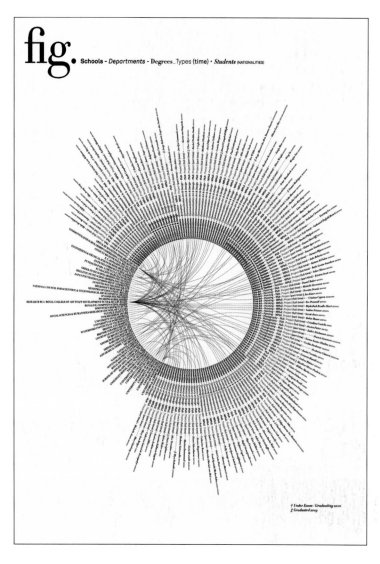

Geometric shapes such as circles, rectangles, or squares inspire a third variety of alternate structure and composition methods. With more complexity than improvised or axial plans, type can rotate concentrically around circles, extend from arcs, or wrap around edges of squares. Many possibilities exist. These atypical structures suit selective projects with text tailored specifically for them. Geometric-inspired layouts exude vibrant first impressions, but be aware of eclipsing communication goals. (Some geometric compositions intentionally and aptly defy typographic design for communication. Artistry or expression, not direct message delivery, drives their function.) Typographic expertise is required to manage such formats. Be attentive to overall composition (macrotypography) and typesetting essentials (microtypography). Seek similar quality on both levels. Avoid forcing type into geometric shapes or awkward arrangements. It sacrifices typeface integrity and can hamper readability. Smart decisions and settings, as well as heightened sensitivity, are essential.

Radial structures make dynamic impressions. Lines of type extend from and revolve around a central core. This poster visualizes the connections between Royal College of Art research students and funding agencies, as well as academic and industry partners. Sans serif Akkurat pairs with serif Didot to order information.

———
KARIN VON OMPTEDA
PETER CRNOKRAK

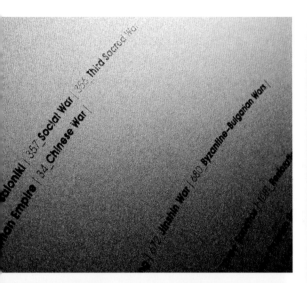

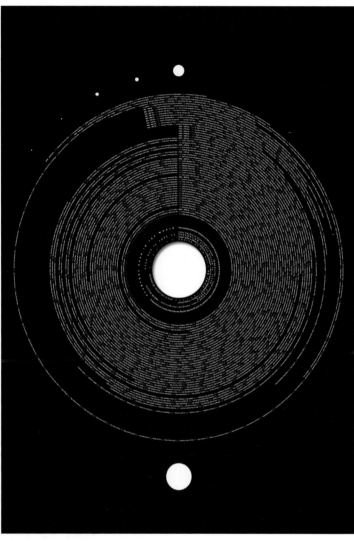

Everyone Ever in the World is a rotational
structure in which type (Avant Garde Gothic)
forms concentric circles, meaning all share
a common center. It is a self-initiated poster
described as "a visual representation of the
number of people [who] lived versus [being]
killed in wars, massacres, and genocide
during the recorded history of humankind."

———
THE LUXURY OF PROTEST

A

APPENDICES

APPENDICES
Readings

A *About Face:*
Reviving the Rules of Typography
David Jury
RotoVision S A

Alphabet:
The History, Evolution, and Design
of the Letters We Use Today
Allen Haley
Watson-Guptill

The Alphabetic Labyrinth:
The Letters in History and Imagination
Johanna Drucker
Thames and Hudson

American Wood Type: 1828–1900
Notes on the Evolution of
Decorated and Large Types
Rob Roy Kelly
Liber Apertus Press

Anatomy of a Typeface
Alexander S. Lawson
David R. Godine

An A–Z of Type Designers
Neil Macmillan
Laurence King Publishing Ltd

C *The Chicago Manual of Style*
University of Chicago Press

The Complete Manual of Typography:
A Guide to Setting Perfect Type
James Felici
Adobe Press

Counterpunch:
Making Type in the Sixteenth Century,
Designing Typefaces Now
Fred Smeijers
Hyphen Press

D *Dangerous Curves:*
Mastering Logotype Design
Doyald Young
Delphi Press

Design Elements: Form & Space
Dennis M. Puhalla, Ph.D.
Rockport Publishers

Designing Type
Karen Cheng
Yale University Press

Designing with Type:
The Essential Guide to Typography
James Craig
Watson-Guptill

Detail in Typography
Jost Hochuli
Hyphen Press

E *The Education of a Typographer*
Steven Heller, ed.
Allworth Press

The Elements of Typographic Style
Robert Bringhurst
Hartley and Marks

An Essay on Typography
Eric Gill
David R. Godine

Experimental Typography
Rob Carter
RotoVision S A

Explorations in Typography:
Mastering the Art of Fine Typesetting
Carolina De Bartolo
with Erik Spiekermann
101 Editions, L L C

F *Finer Points in the Spacing*
and Arrangement of Type
Geoffrey Dowding
Hartley and Marks

Font. The SourceBook
Nadine Monem
Black Dog Publishing

Fonts & Logos:
Font Analysis, Logotype Design,
Typography, Type Comparison
Doyald Young
Delphi Press

The Form of the Book:
Essays on the Morality of Good Design
Jan Tschichold
Hartley and Marks

From Gutenberg to OpenType:
An Illustrated History of Type
from the Earliest Letterforms
to the Latest Digital Fonts
Robin Dodd
Hartley and Marks

G Geometry of Design:
Studies in Proportion
and Composition
Kimberly Elam
Princeton Architectural Press

Grid Systems in Graphic Design
Josef Müller-Brockmann
Arthur Niggli

The Gutenberg Galaxy:
The Making of Typographic Man
Marshall McLuhan
University of Toronto Press

H A History of Writing from
Hieroglyph to Multimedia
Anne-Marie Christin
Flammarion

How Typography Happens
Ruari McLean
Oak Knoll Press

I An Introduction to the
History of Printing Types
Geoffrey Dowding
Oak Knoll Press

J Jan Tschichold:
A Life in Typography
Ruari McLean
Princeton Architectural Press

Just My Type:
A Book About Fonts
Simon Garfield
Gotham Books

L Letter Forms
Stanley Morison
Hartley and Marks

Letter Fountain
Joep Pohlen
Taschen

Letter Perfect:
The Art of Modernist Typography
1896–1953
David Ryan
Pomegranate Communications

Letter Perfect:
The Marvelous History of
Our Alphabet from A to Z
David Sacks
Broadway Books

Letter by Letter
Laurent Pflughaupt
Princeton Architectural Press

Lettering and Type:
Creating Letters
and Designing Typefaces
Bruce Willen
Nolen Strals
Princeton Architectural Press

Letterletter
Gerrit Noordzij
Hartley and Marks

Letters of Credit:
A View of Type Design
Walter Tracy
David R. Godine

Letterwork:
Creative Letterforms in Graphic Design
Brody Neuenschwander
Phaidon Press

The Liberated Page
Herbert Spencer
Bedford Press

Logotypes & Letterforms:
Handlettered Logotypes and
Typographic Considerations
Doyald Young
Design Press

M Making and Breaking the Grid
Tim Samara
Rockport Publishers

Manuale Typographicum
Hermann Zapf
M I T Press

Manuel français de
typographie moderne
Francis Thibaudeau
Au Bureau de l'Édition

Modern Typography:
An Essay in Critical History
Robin Kinross
Hyphen Press

Moving Type:
Designing for Time and Space
Jeff Bellantoni
Matt Woolman
RotoVision S A

Type and Image:
The Language of Graphic Design
Philip B. Meggs
John Wiley and Sons

Type and Typography
Phil Baines
Andrew Halsam
Watson-Guptill

Type and Typography:
The Designer's Type Book
Ben Rosen
Van Nostrand Reinhold Company

Typeface: Classic Typography
for Contemporary Design
Tamye Riggs
James Grieshaber
Princeton Architectural Press

Typeforms: A History
Alan Bartram
Oak Knoll Press

Typographers on Type:
An Illustrated Anthology from
William Morris to the Present Day
Ruari McLean, ed.
W. W. Norton

Typographic Design:
Form and Communication
Rob Carter
Ben Day
Philip Meggs
John Wiley and Sons

The Typographic Desk Reference
Theodore Rosendorf
Oak Knoll Press

Typographic Specimens:
The Great Typefaces
Rob Carter
Philip Meggs
John Wiley and Sons

Typographic Systems of Design
Kimberly Elam
Princeton Architectural Press

Typography: A Manual of Design
Emil Ruder
Arthur Niggli

Typography:
An Encyclopedic Survey of
Type Design and Techniques
Throughout History
Fiedrich Friedl
Nicolaus Ott
Bernard Stein
Black Dog & Leventhal Publishers

Typography:
Formation + Transformation
Willi Kunz
Arthur Niggli

Typography:
Macro + Microaesthetics
Willi Kunz
Arthur Niggli

Typography Referenced
Allan Haley, Richard Poulin,
Jason Tselentis, Gerry Leonidas,
Tony Seddon, Ina Saltz, and
Kathyrn Henderson
Rockport Publishers

Typography Workbook
Tim Samara
Rockport Publishers

U U&lc:
Influencing Design and Typography
John D. Berry
Mark Batty Publisher

The Univers
Adrian Frutiger
Verlag

Unjustified Texts:
Perspectives on Typography
Robin Kinross
Hyphen Press

V The Visible Word:
Experimental Typography and Modern Art,
1909–1923
Johanna Drucker
University of Chicago Press

W While You're Reading
Gerard Unger
Mark Batty Publisher

Wolfgang Weingart: Typography
Wolfgang Weingart
Lars Müller Publishers

A *Addis Creson*
2515 Ninth St.
Berkeley, CA 94710
USA
positivechange@addiscreson.com
addiscreson.com

Despina Aeraki
Giota Kokkosi
47 Troias str.
11251 Athens
Greece
info@aeraki.gr
aeraki.gr

Kristín Agnarsdóttir
2155 Ashby Ave.
Berkeley, CA 94705
USA
kristinagnars@gmail.com
dottirdesign.com

Alphabetical
6 Printing House Yard
Shoreditch, London E27PR
UK
i@alphabetical.com
alphabeticalstudio.com

August Bureau
hello@augustbureau.com
augustbureau.com

B *Dan Becker*
33 Pearl St., #14
San Francisco, CA 94103
USA
beckerdg@gmail.com
dan-becker.com

Bløk Design
287 MacPherson Ave., Suite 201
Toronto, Ontario M4V 1A4
Canada
ve@blokdesign.com
blokdesign.com

David Březina
Potocká 42
Brno 623 00
Czech Republic
brezina@davi.cz
davi.cz

Tyler Brooks
612 Broderick St.
San Francisco, CA 94117
USA
tyler.a.brooks@gmail.com

C *Antonio Carusone*
acarusone@mac.com

Paula Chang
1124 Palm Dr.
Burlingame, CA 94010
USA
chang.paula@gmail.com
quitecurious.com

Karen Cheng
Kristine Matthews
University of Washington
Design Division, Box 353440
Seattle, WA 98112
USA
kcheng@uw.edu
design.washington.edu

Cheng Design
2433 East Aloha St.
Seattle, WA 98112
USA
karen@cheng-design.com
cheng-design.com

Collective Approach
info@collectiveapproach.com
collectiveapproach.com

Patrick L Crawford
1044 Valencia St., #1
San Francisco, CA 94110
USA
patricklcrawford@gmail.com
patricklcrawford.com

D *Design Sense*
Patteelstraat 24
8900 Ieper (Ypres)
Belgium
info@designsense.be
designsense.be

E *El Studio*
5 New St., Largs, Ayrshire
Scotland KA30 9LL
UK
studio@el-studio.co.uk
el-studio.co.uk

Euro RSCG C&O
2 Allée de Longchamp
Suresnes, 92150
France

F *FBA.*
Av. Emidio Navarro 91
3000–151 Coimbra
Portugal
info@fba.pt
fba.pt

Face.
Vasconcelos 204–B
San Pedro, Nuevo León, 66250
Mexico
hello@designbyface.com
designbyface.com

Foxtrot Bravo Alpha (*F B A*)
638 Tillery
Austin, T X 78702
U S A
yall@foxtrotbravoalpha.com
foxtrotbravoalpha.com

G *G 2 K*
info@g2k.nl
g2k.nl

Galison
28 West 44th St.
New York, N Y 10036
U S A
galison.com

Charles Gibbons
11004 Avalon Dr.
Northborough, M A 01532
U S A
cg@gibbonstype.net
gibbonstype.net

Grip Limited
179 John St., 6th Floor
Toronto, Ontario M 6 G 1 T 8
Canada
griplimited.com

I *idApostle*
336 Liard St.
Stittsville, Ontario
Canada
steve@idapostle.com
idapostle.com

Imagine-cga
The Stables, Ducie St.
Manchester M 1 2 J N
U K
david@imagine-cga.co.uk
imagine-cga.co.uk

Kendra Inman
1520 Andalusia Ave., #5
Venice, C A 90291
U S A
kendra@oneloveorganics.com
oneloveorganics.com

Inventaire
Av. de la Gare 8
1630 Bulle
Switzerland
office@inventaire.ch
inventaire.ch

K *Tomato Košir*
Britof 141
Kranj, 4000
Slovenia
tomato@tomatokosir.com
tomatokosir.com

L *L S D space*
San Andrés 36, 2° Puerta 6
28004 Madrid
Spain
gabriel@lsdspace.com
lsdspace.com

Luke Langhus
407 West 3rd St.
Monona, I A 52159
U S A
lukelanghus@gmail.com

Luxecetera
3433 Lithia Pinecrest Rd., #285
Valrico, F L 33596
U S A
luxecetera.com

The Luxury of Protest
2 Queensdown Rd., Unit 10
London E 5 8 N N
U K
info@theluxuryofprotest.com
theluxuryofprotest.com

M *M I N E* ™
190 Putnam St.
San Francisco, C A 94110
U S A
info@minesf.com
minesf.com

Mirko Ilić Corp.
207 East 32nd St.
New York, N Y 10016
U S A
studio@mirkoilic.com
mirkoilic.com

Monderer Design
2067 Massachusetts Ave., Suite 21
Cambridge, M A 02140
U S A
info@monderer.com
monderer.com

Mucca Design
568 Broadway, Room 504
New York, N Y 10012
U S A
info@muccadesign.com
mucca.com

N *Naden/Mesker Design Co.*
2105 Edina Blvd.
Zion, I L 60099
U S A
mail@namedesignco.com
namedesignco.com

Nelson Associates
Town Hall Buildings, Castle St.
Farnham, Surrey GU9 7ND
UK
info@nelsonassociates.co.uk
nelsonassociates.co.uk

Niedermeier Design
5943 44th Ave. SW
Seattle, WA 98136
USA
kurt@kngraphicdesign.com
kngraphicdesign.com

O Falko Ohlmer
Waterloostrasse 3
22769 Hamburg
Germany
hello@falko-ohlmer.com
falko-ohlmer.com

P Project Projects
161 Bowery, 2nd Floor
New York, NY 10002
USA
project@projectprojects.com
projectprojects.com

R Jesse Reed
1148 Academy Dr.
Youngstown, OH 44505
USA
jesse.middle.reed@gmail.com
jessereedfromohio.com

Rui Ribeiro
34 Lottie Rd., Selly Oak
Birmingham B29 6JZ
UK
ribeiro.r.rui@gmail.com
cofseeing.com

Pete Rossi
topeterossi@gmail.com
pgerossi.co.uk

Rule29
501 Hamilton St.
Geneva, IL 60134
USA
rule29.com

S Sensus Design Factory
Sijecanjska 9
Zagreb, HR–10000
Croatia
nedjeljko.spoljar@zg.t-com.hr
sensusdesignfactory.com

Sergey Shapiro
Akademika Piljugina str. 14–2–595
Moscow 117393
Russia
serjio@fromtheska.ru
fromtheska.ru

Strom Strandell
1444 West Erie, 2D
Chicago, IL 60642
USA
stromstrandell@gmail.com

T take off – media services
Pestalozzistr. 19
34119 Kassel
Germany
info@takeoff-ks.de
takeoff-ks.de

Tore Terrasi
5416 Independence Ave.
Arlington, TX 76017
USA
toreterrasi@yahoo.com
toreterrasi.com

Aggie Toppins
6 East Read St. #500
Baltimore, MD 21202
USA
turbotoppins@gmail.com
aggietoppins.com

V Matthijs van Leeuwen
746 Ridge St.
Newark, NJ 01704
USA
contact@matthijsvanleeuwen.com
matthijsvanleeuwen.com

Karin von Ompteda
2 Queensdown Rd., Unit 10
London E5 8NN
UK
karin.von-ompteda@network.rca.ac.uk
karinvonompteda.com
info@quantitativetype.com
quantitativetype.com

W Akshata Wadekar
12030 Norwell Ct.
Cincinnati, OH 45240
USA
wadekar.akshata@gmail.com

Walk Up Press
194 Court St. #11
Brooklyn, NY 11201
USA
info@walkuppress.com
walkuppress.com

Lance Wilson
elance.wilson@gmail.com
elancewilson.com

APPENDICES
Image Credits

APPENDICES
Acknowledgments & About the Author

THANK YOU

Rockport Publishers, for the opportunity to work together again

All contributors, for making the effort to share your work

Edward and Pamela Cullen, for your steadfast support and love

David Thomas, for your patience and trust

Dennis Puhalla, for your guidance and friendship

Renate Gokl, for your instruction and example

My Students, for your attention and dedication

Family and friends, for your understanding

With sincere gratitude,
Joe Bottoni, Stan Brod, Maren Carpenter Fearing,
Yoshiko Burke, Maureen France, The Grillo Group,
Jonathan Hayes, Sandy McGlasson, Laura Morriss,
Gordon Salchow, Heinz Schenker

Kristin Cullen is a graphic designer, author, and educator
based in Chicago, Illinois. Her work has appeared in national
and international exhibits, as well as publications that include
American Corporate Identity, *Graphic Design USA*, *Graphis
Poster Annual*, *HOW*, and *Print*. Kristin also wrote *Layout
Workbook: A Real-World Guide to Building Pages in Graphic
Design*. She holds a master's of fine arts from the Rhode
Island School of Design and a bachelor's of fine arts from
the University of Illinois at Urbana-Champaign.

Don't miss the other books in the series!

Design Elements
Tim Samara
978–1–59253–261–2

Design Elements: Form & Space
Dennis M. Puhalla, Ph.D.
978–1–59253–700–6

Design Elements: Color Fundamentals
Aaris Sherin
978–1–59253–719–8